CW00672156

History of Russia

An Enthralling Overview of Major Events in Russian History

Free limited time bonus

Stop for a moment. We have a free bonus set up for you. The problem is this: we forget 90% of everything that we read after 7 days. Crazy fact, right? Here's the solution: we've created a printable, 1-page pdf summary for this book that you're reading now. All you have to do to get your free pdf summary is to go to the following website: **https://livetolearn.lpages.co/enthrallinghistory/**

Once you do, it will be intuitive. Enjoy, and thank you!

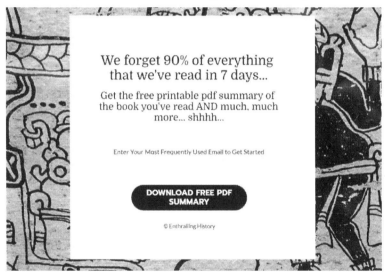

Table of Contents

Introduction

Attempting to document the history of Russia is a formidable task. As the largest country in the world, Russia encompasses almost 11 percent of the world's landmass and is the home of many different cultures. There's a lot of history to cover, and documenting the entire history of Russia would fill a number of books. Russian history contains many controversial and famous figures, such as Catherine the Great, the Romanov family, Vladimir Lenin, and Joseph Stalin. Besides the main events in Russian history, there are also changes in culture, literature, and science that will fascinate any lover of history. A comprehensive guide to Russian history is difficult to compile, but this introductory guide will put you on the right path.

The history of Russia begins with the early Slavic kingdoms, such as the first major Slavic state, Kievan Rus'. According to legend, the state was founded by a Viking named Oleg of Novgorod, but historians dispute this. For years, Kiev (today's Kyiv) acted as the capital of the Slavic state. Prince Vladimir set about ruling the Rurik dynasty and converted many Slavs from paganism to Orthodox Christianity. Unfortunately, Russia was later invaded by the Mongols, who destroyed Moscow and Kiev, the latter of which had become a center of culture and politics in Eastern Europe. These events are the subject of the first part of the book and lay a powerful foundation for the rest of Russian history.

Ivan the Great forced the Mongols out of Russia and established Muscovite rule. While this was initially good news for the Russian people, the Muscovite line produced Ivan the Terrible, who reigned with an iron fist and terrorized the nobility. When he died, Russia was plunged into instability and only began to recover under the Romanov dynasty, which would rule Russia for a little over three hundred years. The second part of this book will explore the rise and fall of the Romanov dynasty. It includes the story of colorful figures like Catherine the Great, Napoleon Bonaparte, and various influential tsars.

Eventually, the Romanov dynasty declined as the world began preparing for the First World War. Russia was rocked by the war, which eventually led to the February Revolution and the October Revolution. Part three of this book will take a look at the climactic events that would have long-lasting effects on modern history.

The Romanov dynasty was replaced by communist leaders who sought to lead Russia into an enlightened and modern era. This eventually led to the formation of the Union of Soviet Socialist Republics (USSR). The USSR brought new economic policies and cultural changes to its people. During this period, Russia fought different wars, including the Great Patriotic War and the Cold War. While the USSR stood for lofty ideals, it eventually stagnated. Despite Russia's stagnation, it was able to emerge as a front-runner during the Space Race and developed an enviable space program.

In time, the USSR was dissolved, and leaders like Boris Yeltsin were able to pioneer a new era in Russian society. The fourth and final part of the book covers the events from the First World War to the controversial reforms brought about by Vladimir Putin.

While the full history of Russia would fill hundreds of books, this comprehensive guide will help readers become acquainted with some of the most important events and time periods in Russian history.

PART ONE: Early Slavic Kingdoms and the Mongol Invasion (800–1480 CE)

Chapter 1: The Early East Slavs and Kievan Rus'

The early Slavs lived in Central and Eastern Europe approximately between the 5th and 10th centuries. Unfortunately, few historical records still exist from the early Slavs, which means a lot of the information about them is saturated with theories and legends. Scholars believe the Slavs originated in Eastern Europe in Polesia (a region that spans parts of modern Central and Eastern Europe).

Map of Polesia.
https://commons.wikimedia.org/wiki/File:Polesia_map_-_topography.jpg

The Byzantine Empire was among the first to acknowledge the Slavs, and their records play a vital part in untangling their mysterious story. In time, the Slavs met the Vikings, who would go on to form Kievan Rus', a vast territory that would eventually form a large part of Russia.

"Barbarian" Enemies of Rome

Slavs are an ethnic group of people who all speak Slavic languages. Writing was only incorporated into the Slavic culture when the Slavs converted to Christianity around the 9th and 10th centuries. Some authors claim the Slavs were nomads, while others suggest they originally lived in states located in forests. It seems the Slavs occupied a large amount of territory and shared common cultural elements instead of being completely united under one ruler. There is a lot of debate over how the early Slavs were organized. Some accounts state the Slavs were ruled by a king, while others suggest they used a primitive form of democracy.

According to archaeological evidence, proto-Slavic cultures lived in parts of modern-day western Poland and Belarus by 1500 BCE. Interestingly, scholars have been able to detect traces of Iranian and Germanic languages in Slavic languages. This means that at some point, the Slavs came into contact with Iranian and Germanic tribes.

Archaeologists have uncovered some clues about early Slavic culture. Apparently, the Slavs worshiped a god named Perun, who was considered the supreme god by some Slavic cultures. Perun was similar to the Norse god Thor, who was a thunder god. Another Slavic god was Yarilo, who was the god of youth and spring. He was a high-ranking god, as was his consort, Lada, the goddess of love. It appears as though these two gods died every year and were resurrected, which would have connected them to fertility.

Pendant of the god Perun.

Historians know the Slavs were enemies of the Romans during the later stages of the Roman Empire. The Romans were biased against all of their enemies and deemed most non-Romans as savage and uncivilized. In the 5th century, the Slavs made it difficult for the Romans to keep their borders along the Balkans. Throughout the century, the Slavs engaged in several campaigns against the Romans. In the 550s CE, the Slavs devastated the region of the Hebrus River and destroyed several cities. After the destruction, the Slavs turned the women and children into slaves but killed all the men. Accounts report that the Slavs wanted to capture Thessalonica but were thwarted by the Roman army. In 585, the Slavs marched on Constantinople, but the Romans were able to drive them off. However, during this time, the Slavs were able to establish permanent footholds in Greece.

In 626, the Slavs joined forces with the Avars and Bulgars and once again set their sights on Constantinople. The Slavs were almost able to accomplish their goal but were repelled by the Romans. Since the Slavs were able to occupy parts of Greece, they would frequently butt heads with the emerging Byzantine Empire.

The Byzantine Empire and the Slavs

The Slavs frequently raided the Byzantine Empire's Danube border. Byzantine writers referred to the Slavs as the "Veneti." The Veneti were divided into two distinct groups: the Sclavenes and the Antes. It is important to note that one Byzantine writer, Procopius of Caesarea, wrote the Sclavenes and Antes spoke the same language. This likely means that while the two groups lived in different areas, they still shared many common traits.

Byzantine historians also reported the Slavs were ruled by the strongest and most cunning among them. Slavic society was dominated by village elders who were viewed as wise men and were tasked with passing their knowledge to the younger generation. The Slavs engaged in raids against the Byzantine Empire, and the Byzantines claimed the Slavs intentionally caused chaos to take over the lands they wanted. Once the Slavs settled into a new territory, they integrated the existing people into their own culture. It appears as though the Slavs originated in Eastern Europe and then slowly migrated to Central Europe and the Balkans, where they incorporated the Scythians, Alans, and Sarmatians into their culture.

This integration allowed the Slavic fighting style, armor, weapons, and warfare to become increasingly diverse. When the Byzantine Empire fell, the Slavs organized themselves into kingdoms and were able to keep the Mongol hordes at bay.

The Khazars

The Khazars were a Turkic people who originated in Central Asia. They eventually converted to Judaism and spread into the Northern Caucasus. As time passed, they controlled a lot of lands in Eastern Europe. During the height of their power, they controlled much of modern-day southern Russia, as well as parts of Kazakhstan, Ukraine, Dagestan, Georgia, and Azerbaijan. They had a mostly peaceful relationship with the Byzantine Empire and helped the Byzantines against the Sassanids. The Khazars likely prevented an Arab invasion of Eastern Europe by fighting against the Arab caliphates.

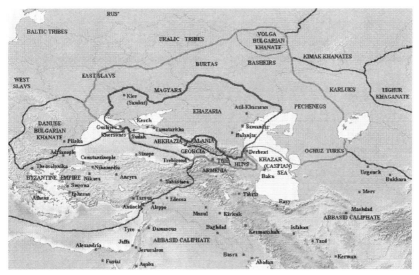

Map showing the Khazar Empire.

It appears as though the Khazars were ruled by a khagan and the bek (or a khagan bek). It is believed the khagan was a spiritual ruler who had limits placed on his power, while the bek controlled the military and administration. According to Arab sources, the khagan typically lived on an island in the Volga River. The khagan had numerous wives, as he received one daughter from each client ruler, but this may be an exaggeration.

The Khazars were located in a prime trading location, as goods were brought through Khazar states from Western Europe to Asia and the East. The Muslim world was forced to trade with Northern Europe through Khazar intermediaries, and the Khazars placed a levy on all goods that went through their borders. The Khazars traded a vast number of goods, namely honey, wool, millet, fish, slaves, and furs. The Khazars also allowed the Radhanites (a guild of Jewish merchants) to use a trade route that went through their empire. This may have led to the Khazars' conversion to Judaism.

Eventually, their alliance with the Byzantine Empire began to collapse in the 900s, and the Byzantines began making alliances with the Rus' and Pechenegs in the hope of isolating the Khazar state further. Khazar imperial power was defeated in the 960s.

Vikings in Russia

It appears as though the Vikings first appeared in Russia in the 6th century. During this time, the Khazars were still ruling, which means the two groups often butted heads. The Vikings might not have been looking to conquer the territory; their initial goal might have been to trade with the people of Eastern Europe. The Norwegians and Danish mostly stayed in Western Europe, but the Swedes began looking further than that and eventually began trading in the Baltic and regions located in modern-day Russia. The Vikings eventually became the rulers of Slavic territories in Novgorod and Kiev. These Vikings were known as the Rus' to the Slavs. The Rus' (they were also referred to as Varangians) associated freely with the Slavs and created a series of clans. Viking princes took control of Kiev (modern-day Kyiv) and Novgorod in the late 800s.

At first, the Khazars had a good relationship with the Rus', and it seems the Rus' were influenced by Khazar culture. The Khazars even allowed the Rus' to use a trading route along the Volga River. However, when the Rus' began attacking Arab lands, the relationship between the Arabs and Khazars began to sour. As a result, the Khazars were forced to end their alliance with the Rus'.

Much of the information about the Rus' and their eventual Slavic state, Kievan Rus', is derived from the *Russian Primary Chronicle*, which was likely completed in 113 CE. While it provides a lot of historical information, many of the stories seem to have been exaggerated or influenced by legends. However, archaeological evidence supports some of the information in the *Chronicle*. According to the *Russian Primary Chronicle*, the region of Kievan Rus' was given to Noah's son, Japheth. This alludes to the Great Flood described in the Bible. For those unfamiliar with the story, a global flood destroyed all of mankind except for the faithful man Noah, who survived along with his wife, his three sons, and his sons' wives.

Accordingly, the Slavs who lived in the land given to Japheth were eventually subdued by the Khazars and the Varangians. In time, the Slavs drove the Varangians away but found the Khazars had become increasingly harsh. The Slavs were unable to govern themselves and decided to appeal to the Varangians for help. The *Chronicle* states the Slavs went to the lands of the Varangians (it doesn't mention where these lands were located) and asked the Varangians to return and rule over the Slavs again. Three noble brothers responded to this appeal.

Three Noble Brothers

The *Russian Primary Chronicle* states that three brothers decided to return to the land of the Slavs and establish themselves as kings. The oldest, Rurik, decided to take the region surrounding Novgorod, while the second, Sineus, chose Beloozero. The final brother, Truvor, chose Izborsk. While many have rejected the *Chronicle*'s claims, some Norse artifacts were found at a site at Novgorod, which means there may be some truth in the *Chronicle*'s reports. Archaeologists have found Scandinavian settlements near the Volkhov River from as early as 750 CE. It doesn't appear as if the Vikings wanted to raid the areas, as there was very little to steal, so it's likely they wanted to take advantage of Russia's resources.

That first settlement experienced a population fluctuation, which adds credence to the *Chronicle*'s claims that the Slavs expelled the Rus' only to ask them to return later. The *Chronicle* continues the story of the three brothers and claims that Sineus and Truvor eventually died, which allowed Rurik to assimilate their regions into his lands. Two of his men, Askold and Dir, were allowed to leave and find their own lands. They were originally supposed to go to Constantinople but found a prosperous city named Kyiv or Kiev (the difference in the spelling results from the English translation of two different languages; Kyiv is the English translation of the Ukrainian word, while Kiev is from Russian). Askold and Dir conquered the city and used it as a base for raids on surrounding cities, which allowed them to amass large amounts of wealth.

In time, Rurik died, leaving behind a young son, Igor. However, Igor was still too young to rule, so Rurik entrusted his son to one of his men, Oleg, who ruled over Rurik's lands.

Prince Oleg of Novgorod

Oleg of Novgorod immediately began expanding the lands he had been given. He conquered surrounding regions and incorporated them into his domain. As his territory kept growing, he eventually found Askold and Dir at Kiev. They had managed to secure massive fortunes for themselves through their frequent raids. Oleg recognized the value of Kiev, but instead of forming an alliance, he managed to get Askold and Dir out of the city and killed them, allowing him to take full control. This made him the founder of Kievan Rus'. According to the *Russian Primary Chronicle*, Oleg became the ruler of Novgorod around 879. By 882, he had captured Kiev and Smolensk. Since Kiev was located in a prime location along the Dnieper River, he made Kiev his capital.

At this time, the Khazars were still a formidable ruling power and demanded tribute from surrounding states. Once Oleg captured Kiev, he began convincing surrounding states and tribes to pay tribute to him instead. Besides Oleg's military victories, he also made several lucrative treaties, including a trade deal with Constantinople. The *Chronicle* also states that Oleg was called Oleg the Priest (or prophet) and details a disturbing prophecy that Oleg received.

According to the prophecy, Oleg was going to be killed by a horse that he owned. Oleg immediately ordered the horse be sent away but made arrangements to make sure it was always well cared for. In time, Oleg became confident in his own reign and scoffed at the prophecy. When he was told his horse had died, he ordered the bones be brought to him. He loudly mocked the prophecy and went to crush the horse's skull beneath his feet, but when he stepped on the skull, he disturbed a snake that had been hiding under it. The snake immediately bit him, and he died from the poison.

Prince Oleg stepping on his horse's skull.

During his reign, Oleg dutifully raised Rurik's son, Igor of Kiev, who became Oleg's successor.

Rise of Kievan Rus'

According to historical sources, the Vikings first visited Constantinople around 830. They must have been impressed by what they saw because they besieged the city in 860 and then again in 907. While the Vikings were powerful enough to present a serious threat to Constantinople, they weren't able to capture the city. In time, the relationship between the Rus' and Constantinople became more positive, and they were able to make trade deals and treaties. The Rus' supplied Constantinople with a steady supply of slaves, honey, and furs, while Constantinople gave the Rus' luxury items in return.

Principalities of Kievan Rus' (1054 CE).

Oleg expanded Kievan Rus' from Kiev to the Dnieper River and had a series of forts that eventually reached the Baltic. This put him in direct opposition with the Khazars, who felt he was encroaching on their territory. While the Khazars were originally allies of the Rus', this relationship eventually soured.

Oleg decided to attack the Khazars. The Byzantines often interfered with this conflict, as it benefited them since the Khazars and Rus' both presented various threats to the Byzantine Empire. According to a historical record called the Schechter Letter, Oleg fought against the Khazar Empire around 941, going up against the Khazar general Pesakh. Oleg lost the fight.

Grand Prince Sviatoslav I of Kiev was responsible for conquering the Khazars. In the 960s, he captured the Khazar strongholds of Tamantarkhan and Sarkel. Finally, the Khazar capital of Atil fell to the Rus'. According to a contemporary source, the Rus' sacked the city so thoroughly that nothing was left. With the Khazars out of the way, the Kievan Rus' state was able to grow to new heights.

Olga of Kiev

While the *Russian Primary Chronicle* provides many helpful details that clarify the history of Kievan Rus', it was also heavily influenced by legends. For example, while the story of Oleg's death is fascinating and entertaining, it is likely based more on fiction than reality. Another figure in the *Chronicle* who fell victim to such exaggeration was Olga of Kiev. She may have been a real person, but it is unlikely that she perpetrated all the acts that are described in the *Chronicle*.

According to the *Chronicle*, Igor of Kiev succeeded Oleg of Novgorod. By that time, Igor had married a woman named Olga. Like Oleg, Igor collected tributes from conquered regions. He was also a good warrior and conquered new lands. However, he became greedy and began charging larger tributes. He became so oppressive that a tribe called the Drevlians decided to assassinate him. Their plot was successful, and Olga was left to take care of their young son, Sviatoslav I. Since Sviatoslav was still too young to rule, Olga ruled as regent in his place.

Olga immediately decided to avenge her husband's murder. The Drevlians decided to opt for diplomacy and sent emissaries to arrange a marriage between Olga and their prince, Mai. Olga tricked the emissaries into getting into a boat, which was then carried around. The unsuspecting emissaries were then thrown into a pit and buried alive. However, Olga wasn't done yet. She invited the Drevlian wise men to visit her. When they arrived, she ordered that they bathe before they came to her. Once they were in the bathhouses, she had the bathhouses set on fire, burning the wise men alive. Finally, she claimed she would forgive the Drevlians if they arranged a funeral feast in Igor's honor. They agreed, and at the feast, everyone ate well and got drunk. As soon as the Drevlians were inebriated, Olga ordered her men to kill them all.

A painting of Olga of Kiev's baptism by Sergei Kirillov.

Sergei Kirillov, CC BY-SA 3.0 <https://creativecommons.org/licenses/by-sa/3.0>, via Wikimedia Commons; https://commons.wikimedia.org/wiki/File:Kirillov_knyaginya_olga.jpg

The Drevlians realized Olga was never going to spare them and retreated to the city of Iskorosten. Olga besieged the city but was unable to capture it. Eventually, she promised to stop attacking the city if each household gave her three pigeons and sparrows. The Drevlians complied and gave her the birds. Once she had her tribute, she and her soldiers attached hot sulfur threads to the birds and released them. The birds returned to their nests in the houses of the city. The city caught fire, and Olga either killed or enslaved the survivors.

While most of Olga's story is rooted in legend, the real Olga might have played a part in spreading Christianity throughout Kievan Rus'. The Christian Church later denied all the violent parts of Olga's history and made her a saint due to her missionary work. Despite Olga's efforts, Vladimir the Great would be the one to turn Kievan Rus' from paganism to Orthodox Christianity.

Chapter 2: The Christianization of Kievan Rus' and the Mongol Invasion (980–1340)

When the Vikings arrived in Russia initially, they likely wanted to establish trade routes with the Slavs and other cultures. However, in time, the Vikings became known as the Rus', and they set up Kievan Rus', which became a dominant power in the region. With the fall of the Khazars, Kievan Rus' became increasingly powerful. They exacted tribute from the Slavs, and their Eastern Roman neighbors viewed them as "barbarians." Efforts were made to convert the Rus' to Christianity, but that only came to fruition through the work of Prince Vladimir I.

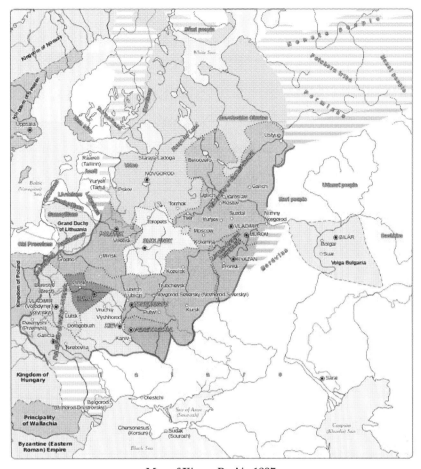

Map of Kievan Rus' in 1237.

The Eastern Orthodox Church had an indelible effect on Slavic culture. Christianity wouldn't be the only new influence on the Slavs and Rus', as a new threat loomed in the East. The Mongols eventually overran Kievan Rus' and turned it into a part of the Golden Horde. In time, the Mongols would be driven out of Russia, but the Mongol invasion would have lasting consequences on Russian history.

Prince Vladimir I

Prince Vladimir was the youngest son of Sviatoslav, the son of the famous Olga of Kiev. Sviatoslav appointed his oldest son, Yaropolk, as the heir to Kiev, while Vladimir was appointed as the prince of Novgorod around 969. A few years later, Sviatoslav died, and the kingdom descended into a period of political instability. Tensions between the brothers escalated until Yaropolk murdered his younger brother Oleg around 976. Vladimir was able to escape to Scandinavia and avoided the same fate.

Vladimir I.
https://commons.wikimedia.org/wiki/File:Vladimir_I_The_Saint.jpg

Thankfully, Vladimir had family in Norway, and the ruler of Norway, Haakon Sigurdsson, took in Vladimir. Together, they plotted against Yaropolk. Vladimir was able to return in 978 and defeat his brother. He had Yaropolk executed on the charge of treason and was able to gain control of his father's kingdom. As the new ruler of Kievan Rus', Vladimir looked for ways to strengthen and expand his territory. According to records, he spent a decade fortifying his borders and strengthening his army. During this time, Kievan Rus' was still primarily pagan. According to the *Russian Primary Chronicle*, Vladimir decided to send envoys to neighboring countries to investigate their religions. The thunder god, Perun, was massively popular in Kievan Rus' and had several shrines and cults that worshiped him. When the envoys returned, they reported the Orthodox Christian religion practiced in Constantinople was impressive, which may have aided in Vladimir's decision to convert to Christianity.

Orthodox Christianity

There are three main groups of Christianity, namely the Orthodox Church, the Roman Catholics, and the Protestants. Most Orthodox churches are either self-governing or have their own head but are united through tradition and theology. Many Orthodox churches have incorporated elements of Middle Eastern, Greek, Slavic, and Russian culture. A lot of Orthodox tradition is based on geography, which means many of the churches are unique and reflect local cultures and traditions. Orthodox Christianity developed from the Christianity practiced by the Eastern Roman Empire. The Orthodox churches share many similarities with other Christian churches, namely the belief that Jesus Christ was God himself and the resurrection and crucifixion of Jesus. However, there are a few notable differences in the Orthodox theology and way of living when compared to other Christian churches.

There are many different Orthodox churches, such as the Eastern Orthodox Church, which traditionally was led by the patriarch of Constantinople. However, most Orthodox churches have their own patriarchs or are led by archbishops. Originally, there was no difference between the Eastern and Western churches; however, over the centuries, schisms developed, with Christian doctrines being decided through various councils. There were five main patriarchal sees; they were located in Rome, Alexandria, Constantinople, Jerusalem, and Antioch. After the split from Rome, Orthodox Christianity became known as the "Eastern" church and became the main Christian force in Asia Minor, Russia, the eastern Mediterranean, and the Balkans.

Around 787, the Western and Eastern churches were almost completely divided. The Eastern Church chafed at the Western

Church's attempt to claim the papacy had the right to control both churches. There were also differences in opinion regarding various theological matters. Most Orthodox believe the great split between Western and Eastern Christianity occurred during the sack of Constantinople during the Fourth Crusade in 1204. The sacking eventually allowed Muslim Ottomans to take control of the historic city in 1453. This capital offense was never forgiven by the Eastern Orthodox Church and cemented the massive gap between the Eastern Church and Rome (the seat of power of the Western Church.

The Baptism of Kiev

There are various versions of how the Rus' was converted to Christianity. One version of events centers around the claim that Prince Vladimir's envoys returned from investigating the religions of surrounding territories and reported on the grandeur of the Orthodox Church. The envoys said the festivities and churches in Constantinople were the most beautiful they had ever seen. These reports convinced Prince Vladimir to adopt the new religion due to the church's beauty and prestige.

However, others claimed that Basil II of Byzantine faced an uprising near Constantinople and needed an ally. He approached Prince Vladimir, who used the situation to demand a royal marriage alliance with Constantinople. To sweeten the deal, Vladimir promised to convert the Rus' in return for the marriage alliance. Another version states that Vladimir fell in love with Basil II's sister, Anna, and converted to Christianity to gain her hand in marriage.

While scholars may never know the real reason for Vladimir's conversion, they know he brought his new wife with him to Kiev in 988. There was a marked difference in Vladimir, as he immediately destroyed all the local pagan temples. He then went on to build the Church of the Tithes, which was the first stone church in Kiev. Kievan Rus' also enjoyed a long-lasting alliance with the Byzantine Empire.

Vladimir didn't stop with the construction of the church. Upon his return to Kiev in 988, he had his twelve sons and other officials baptized. All the citizens of Kiev were summoned to the banks of the Dnieper River, where they were baptized while Orthodox priests prayed over the scene. These actions were meant to turn

Orthodoxy into the new state religion, and the mass baptism became known as the "Baptism of Kiev."

Despite Vladimir's efforts, many communities within Kievan Rus' strongly opposed the new religion, which led to many brutal and violent uprisings. Vladimir died around 1015 and became the figurehead of Russian Orthodoxy. After his death, parts of his body were sent to various churches to serve as holy relics.

The Rise of the Mongols

Like so many other states, Kievan Rus' was only as strong as its rulers. In 1054, Yaroslav the Wise died, and Kievan Rus' was left without its great leader. As a result, the state began to break apart as smaller factions struggled for power. For decades, princes squabbled over territories, which weakened their power. As power was divided between local principalities, cities and territories were left to fend for themselves. To make matters worse, the Byzantine Empire was weakening, so Kievan Rus' couldn't rely on its strongest ally. All of these factors would lead to a much more serious threat: the Mongols.

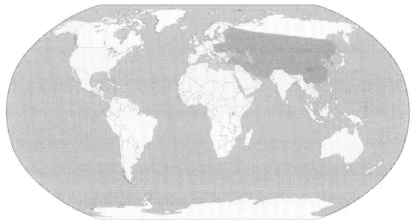

Map of the great Mongol Empire.

Canuckguy and many others, CC BY-SA 4.0 <https://creativecommons.org/licenses/by-sa/4.0>, via Wikimedia Commons; https://commons.wikimedia.org/wiki/File:Great_Mongol_Empire_map.svg

The Mongol Empire was founded by the formidable Genghis Khan and lasted from 1206 to 1368. During that time, it ruled over most of Eurasia. The Mongols had a gigantic army of trained soldiers and the most advanced warfare technology of the time at their disposal. Before the rise of Genghis Khan, the Mongols were forced to maintain a nomadic lifestyle, as their farms and flocks required a steady supply of grass and water. Since droughts and famines were common, the Mongols lived with frequent insecurity.

In 1206, Genghis Khan (previously known as Temüjin, the son of a local chieftain) assumed power and united the Mongol tribes. He reformed laws, established a new type of government, improved trade, and encouraged the advancement of technology, such as leather armor, gunpowder, stirrups, and composite bows. Genghis Khan also embraced a policy of religious freedom.

The Mongol army quickly became incredibly successful. They engaged in psychological warfare, built up large arsenals, and used guerilla warfare tactics, such as hit-and-runs and arrow storms. Thanks to a policy of aggressive expansion, the Mongol Empire's borders quickly expanded. As the Mongol army marched, it spread terror, as reports of their brutal tactics spread throughout surrounding territories. However, the Mongol Empire also fostered a brief period of peace, which allowed for new trading opportunities and safe traveling.

Invasion of Kievan Rus'

During the period of political instability in the 12th century in Kievan Rus', the fractured kingdom was forced to face the incredibly successful and feared Mongol army. Once Central Asia had been united under Mongol rule, the Mongols began looking for new opportunities. They quickly set their sights on Kievan Rus'. In 1223, the Mongol army attacked Kievan Rus' which led to the Battle of the Kalka River. The battle ended with the execution of Mstislav III of Kiev. Kievan Rus' lost a significant portion of its army, and the defeat severely weakened the already struggling state.

After the Mongols' resounding victory at the Battle of the Kalka River, the Mongol army returned to Asia to rejoin Genghis Khan. The Rus' lived in fear of the Mongol forces, which proved to be well-founded as the Mongols returned in 1237. Batu Khan, one of Genghis Khan's grandsons, led the Mongol forces into Kievan Rus' and burned down Kolomna and Moscow. Between 1237 and 1238, he attacked each principality in Kievan Rus'. There was such widespread destruction that thousands of Rus' were forced to flee to the harsh north, where they struggled to make a living due to the scarcity of resources. Very few cities were spared during the invasion. In 1240, Batu Khan finally captured the city of Kiev, and his victory over Kievan Rus' was complete.

The Tatars and the Golden Horde

The European territories that belonged to the Mongol Empire were called the Golden Horde. Mongol tradition states that before Genghis Khan died, he left his empire to his four sons. His son Jochi was allowed to rule the lands around and beyond the Ural Mountains. Later, Jochi's son, Batu Khan, would establish the Golden Horde. Another one of Genghis Khan's sons, Ögedei Khan, ordered the Mongol army to invade Europe, but Batu Khan finished the job.

Once Kievan Rus' had been defeated, the Mongols marched westward to defeat the Polish and Hungarians. The rest of Europe was spared since Ögedei died soon after the defeat of the Hungarian army at the Battle of Mohi (also known as the Battle of the Sajó River). While the Golden Horde remained a fixed Mongolian territory for the next two centuries, the Mongol army never got that far into Europe again. However, the Mongols left a lasting mark on Europe, with the Europeans calling the Mongols "Tatars." This was likely due to the fact that one Mongol clan was called the Tatars, but it also referred to Tartarus, which was the deepest part of the underworld. It was believed the Mongols had arrived straight from hell to wreak havoc on Europe.

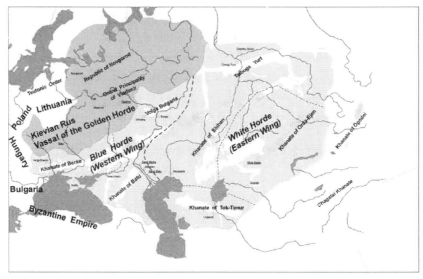

Map of the Golden Horde.

Afil, CC BY-SA 3.0 <https://creativecommons.org/licenses/by-sa/3.0>, via Wikimedia Commons; https://commons.wikimedia.org/wiki/File:Golden_Horde_2.png

After the Mongols took control of Kievan Rus', they built their capital at Sarai, which was located near the Volga River. Russian princes were then forced to pay tribute to the Mongols. Despite the harsh realities of the Mongol invasion, the period of the Tatar yoke (which refers to the economic and cultural rule of the Mongols) was surprisingly peaceful. The Mongols didn't force the Rus' to convert or adopt Mongolian practices. The Rus' were largely left in peace as long as they paid their taxes.

Alexander Nevsky

Alexander Nevsky was born in 1221 and was the prince of Novgorod and Kiev and the grand prince of Vladimir. For years, the Novgorodians had been encroaching on Swedish land in Finnish territory, which led to a Swedish invasion in 1240. Alexander was able to defeat the Swedes, which earned him the honorific of "Nevsky." (Nevsky means "of Neva," referring to his victory in the Battle of Neva.) However, his military prowess didn't hold lasting merit, as the Novgorodians expelled him for getting involved in city affairs.

Alexander Nevsky.
Unknown author, CC BY 4.0 <https://creativecommons.org/licenses/by/4.0>, via Wikimedia Commons; https://commons.wikimedia.org/wiki/File:Alexander_Nevsky-0.jpg

Soon after the Swedish invasion, the pope of the time, Pope Gregory IX, convinced the Teutonic Knights (a Catholic-sanctioned military society that was originally formed to protect and help Christians who made pilgrimages to the Holy Land) to "Christianize" the Baltic. This would prove to be an ironic move since the territories were already predominantly Christian. Alexander was asked to return to Novgorod to defeat this new threat. During a battle on the frozen waters of Lake Peipus in 1242, Alexander defeated the Teutonic Knights.

Unfortunately, the Mongol armies were already in Kievan Rus' and were quickly conquering many Russian principalities. Alexander's father submitted to the Mongol rulers in 1246 but died soon after. Alexander and his brother Andrew appealed to Batu Khan to help them settle the matter of succession. However, since Alexander was Batu's favorite, the great khan made Andrew the grand prince (at the time, the great khan was displeased with Batu

Khan). Andrew tried to conspire against the Mongols, but Alexander revealed the plot to Batu Khan's son, who retaliated and defeated Andrew. Alexander was then appointed as the grand prince.

Alexander chose to pay tribute to the Mongols instead of trying to defeat them, which drew heavy criticism from his peers and the Rus'. While many viewed Alexander's acceptance of Mongol rule as cowardly, he was able to rebuild Russian infrastructure by building churches and fortifications and passing laws. This would not have been possible if he had been deposed by the Mongols.

Alexander continued to protect Kievan Rus' during his reign. He quelled rebellions before the Mongols could react brutally and managed to get the Rus' exempted from a military draft. Alexander's actions garnered support from the Russian Orthodox Church, and he was declared a saint in 1547. Once Alexander died, Kievan Rus' quickly splintered into principalities, but his son, Daniel, was able to establish the house of Moscow.

Impact of the Mongol Invasion

Kievan Rus' was left in a state of ruin after the onslaught of the Mongol invasion, and years of forced taxation meant the Rus' were unable to repair their cities. The Rus' focused on rebuilding Kiev and Pskov, but it took years before the cities were restored. In the meantime, new cities, such as Tver and Moscow, were able to flourish. Novgorod also managed to escape most of the destruction and continued to prosper.

While the years under the Tatar yoke were relatively peaceful, the Rus' still lived with the constant threat of invasion, which happened a few times and always led to heavy burdens for the local population since they were forced to repair the destruction.

The Tatars also built a massive postal road system and introduced new military tactics and organizational methods. Over the years, Mongolian culture began to affect local populations. Russian noblemen began adopting the Mongolian language and changed their names. These cultural elements would have linguistic and aesthetic influences on Russian culture. The Mongol rule also caused the split between the East Slavs and led to the formation of three modern nations: Russia, Belarus, and Ukraine.

By the 14th century, some Mongol leaders had converted to Islam, with rulers of the Golden Horde either practicing Buddhism or Mongolian pagan beliefs. When the Black Death struck in the 14th century, the Golden Horde was severely weakened, and matters were worsened by the outbreak of a civil war. Between 1359 and 1382, the Mongol grip began to weaken on Eastern Europe. In 1380, the Russians were able to secure their first major victory against the Mongols at the Battle of Kulikovo. Eventually, the Golden Horde splintered into distinct khanates, which would slowly be forced into extinction.

Rise of Moscow

In the early years of Russia's history, Moscow was a relatively small trading post that belonged to the principality of Vladimir-Suzdal. In the years of Mongol rule, Moscow was sheltered in the north and mostly spared from the near-constant power struggles and raids that crippled other Russian cities. Cities like Kiev financially struggled since they were forced to rebuild after destructive Mongol raids.

Around 1288, Ivan I was born. He would later become the prince of Moscow and convince many people to move to the city since it was comparatively safer than other cities in Russia. Thanks to Ivan I's savvy politics, he was able to turn Moscow into a prosperous and safe city during the instability of Mongolian leadership. During this time, Moscow became the seat of power of the Russian Orthodox Church.

PART TWO: The Rise of the Russian Empire (1480–1917 CE)

Chapter 3: From the Grand Duchy of Moscow to Peter the Great

When the Mongols invaded Kievan Rus', they ripped through the territory as if nothing could stop them. Kievan Rus' was then turned into the Golden Horde, the European part of the extensive Mongol Empire. The two centuries of Mongol rule are perceived as relatively peaceful, but the Rus' lived in near-constant fear of destructive raids, which would result in expensive damage. Finally, as the Mongol Empire weakened, the Rus' were able to take back their lands, which was largely possible due to the efforts of Ivan III, who would become the "Grand Duke of all the Russias" and Ivan the Great.

Ivan the Great unified Russia and established Moscow as an important Russian city. However, not all his descendants would follow his example, as his grandson, Ivan IV, would become one of the most feared rulers in history and earn the title "Ivan the Terrible." Eventually, the Romanovs took the throne and established an enduring dynasty that would produce the likes of Peter the Great.

Ivan the Great

Ivan III was born in 1440 to Vasili II of Russia. In 1450, Ivan became co-regent with his father and finally succeeded his father in 1462. He proved to be a cautious ruler but had the goal of unifying the Russian states. For decades, Moscow had been a Mongol ally. The city was perched along profitable trade routes between the Volga River and Novgorod. This advantageous geographical position allowed Moscow to flourish, and Ivan III's predecessors were able to greatly expand Moscow's borders. However, Ivan III wasn't satisfied with Moscow's position and decided to find a way to end Mongol rule over the city.

In 1476, he refused to pay the normal tribute to the Mongols. Four years later, Khan Ahmed attacked the city but was forced to retreat to the inner part of the Mongol Empire. By that point, the Mongol Empire was fractured and divided, which meant the Mongol rulers were unable to keep their hold on the Golden Horde.

Ivan III of Russia.
https://commons.wikimedia.org/wiki/File:Ivan_III_of_Russia_(Granovitaya_palata,_1881-2).jpg

Once the Mongols were no longer a problem, Ivan III set his sights on unifying Russia. For years, Moscow and Novgorod had been enemies, but Ivan III was able to defeat the rival city and bring it under his rule. In time, he was able to gain control of Yaroslav, Rostov, Vyatka, and Tver, which brought an end to the autonomous rule of distinct Russian principalities.

Ivan III also made an alliance with the Russian Orthodox Church, which increased his power. The former autonomous Russian princes became part of the nobility, and if a conquered state rebelled, members of its royal family were taken to Moscow or sent to distant lands, which effectively ended most rebellions. Ivan III also created a new legal code called the Muscovite Sudebnik. He later went on to marry Sophia Paleologue of Constantinople, who brought many Byzantine influences into the Russian court.

Ivan the Great was determined to turn Moscow into the next Constantinople. He invited master craftsmen to Moscow and oversaw the construction of many lavish buildings like cathedrals and palaces. Previously, Russia had been ruled through patriarchal systems of governments that were heavily influenced by members of the nobility called boyars. However, Ivan III introduced an autocratic system of government similar to the Byzantine system and made the position of monarch sacred. Boyars were reduced to ministers who depended heavily on the king's will, which sowed seeds of discord among the nobility. Ivan III died in 1505, leaving his son, Vasili III, as the new ruler of Moscow.

Vasili III

Before Ivan III's marriage to Sophia Paleologue, he was married to Maria of Tver. When she died in 1467, Ivan III married Sophia Paleologue, the niece of the last Byzantine emperor, Constantine XI. At first, the condition of their marriage was that Maria's child would inherit the throne. However, Sophia had considerable influence over her husband and encouraged his imperialistic ideals. She was known for being a formidable woman, and it was her son, Vasili III, who inherited Ivan III's throne instead of Maria of Tver's son, Ivan the Young.

Vasili III was born in 1479 and inherited the Muscovite state in 1505. He expanded Moscow's borders by conquering Volokolamsk, Ryazan, Novgorod-Seversky, Pskov, and Smolensk.

The capture of Smolensk was one of his greatest achievements since it was Lithuania's stronghold. While Vasili III's military and political feats were impressive, he was known for being an oppressive ruler. He brutally punished anyone who disobeyed him and cut the power of the boyars, especially those who came from conquered principalities. Vasili III died in 1533, leaving behind his three-year-old son, who would eventually succeed him and become Ivan the Terrible.

Ivan the Terrible

Ivan IV was only eight years old when his mother died, leaving him and his deaf-mute brother Yuri in the hands of the nobility, who resented Ivan's father and grandfather for greatly reducing their power. Some reports claim that Ivan and Yuri were treated terribly as children and were frequently left without food or proper clothes. This treatment at the hands of the nobility fostered a deep mistrust and eventual hatred of the nobles in Ivan. Apparently, when he was thirteen, Ivan IV was with the Shuisky family. In 1453, while at a feast, Ivan had the most powerful Shuisky, Prince Andrei, arrested for mismanaging the country. Prince Andrei was put to death shortly after, likely beaten to death by his jailers.

Ivan IV of Russia.
https://commons.wikimedia.org/wiki/File:Ivan_the_Terrible_(cropped).JPG

When he was sixteen, Ivan IV was crowned "Tsar of all Russias." Shortly thereafter, he married Anastasia Romanovna. The marriage cemented his alliance with the formidable Romanov family. While Ivan IV gained an infamous reputation, the early years of his rule went relatively well. He established a standing army and a Russian parliament. He brought the first printing press to Russia, constructed St. Basil's Cathedral in Moscow, and established new church regulations.

Unfortunately, in the 1560s, Russia went through a difficult time due to Tatar invasions, a sea blockade initiated by the Swedes and Poles, and a terrible drought. To make matters worse, Anastasia died in 1560, likely from poison. These events caused Ivan IV to struggle mentally, and he fled from Moscow in 1564. He was persuaded to return on the condition he would be granted absolute power. Ivan IV went on to harass the boyars by executing, exiling, and forcibly removing them from their positions of power.

Despite his increasing reputation as a mentally unstable leader, he had many impressive achievements. He made a profitable trade agreement with England and defeated the Kazan Khanate, the Crimean horde, and many Siberian regions. Unfortunately, he also made several reckless decisions, such as the Livonian War, which lasted for twenty-four years and drained Russia of necessary resources. During the war, Russia fought against the Polish-Lithuanian Commonwealth and the Swedish Empire.

Ivan IV died in 1584 of a stroke. Ivan IV had murdered his eldest son in a fit of passion, so the throne passed to Feodor Ivanovich, a man who was not mentally capable of ruling.

Time of Troubles

Unfortunately, Feodor Ivanovich died in 1598 without an heir, which left Russia in a state of dynastic crisis. The Zemsky Sobor, or Great National Assembly, appointed Boris Godunov as Feodor's successor. According to reports, Feodor had been mentally challenged, and Boris was the boyar who effectively assisted Feodor during his reign. However, many other noble families viewed Boris as low-ranking before his appointment as tsar and refused to follow him. Thus, Boris had a short and troubled reign, which ended in 1605.

From 1601 to 1603, a devastating famine afflicted Russia and caused the deaths of about two million Russians. The famine was caused by a volcanic eruption in Peru a year earlier. Unfortunately, the eruption caused temperatures to remain colder than usual during the day and plummeted to freezing at night, which killed vast amounts of crops. Residents desperately went to Moscow, looking for food while straining the city's resources.

Once the famine was over, things only got worse. Before Boris's reign, Feodor Ivanovich's younger brother had died after being reportedly stabbed (it is not known whether it was self-inflicted). However, many believed Feodor's younger brother, Dmitri, had escaped. As a result, a few pretenders came forward. For years, Russia was beset by the False Dmitris, with pretenders rising up and gaining followers to invade Russia. The first pretender was supported by the Lithuanians, Cossacks, and Russian exiles. False Dimitri I ascended to the throne in 1605 after Boris's death and the short reign of his son. However, Vasili Shuisky dethroned and killed the pretender before taking the throne for himself. He ruled from 1606 to 1610.

During Shuisky's rule, another false Dimitri appeared with the support of the Poles and Lithuanians. Around 1605, the Polish-Muscovite War began, lasting until 1618 and further straining Moscow's resources. Meanwhile, the boyars squabbled amongst themselves as they tried to take power for themselves.

Finally, Michael Romanov was elected as the tsar of Russia in 1613 by the Grand National Assembly.

Michael I Romanov

Michael I was born in 1596 to an important boyar named Feodor Nikitich Romanov, who had been exiled by Boris Godunov in 1600. However, the Romanovs rose to prominence during the Time of Troubles. Feodor had been forced to take monastic vows and became known as Patriarch Filaret. Michael was a popular choice for the throne since he was distantly related to Ivan the Terrible and Feodor Romanov. While the boyars were satisfied with the outcome, Michael's future was incredibly uncertain due to the political atmosphere that lingered due to the Time of Troubles.

Michael I proved to be a competent leader who managed to reinvigorate Moscow. He also developed the Razryadny Prikaz (provincial administration office) and the Posolsky Prikaz (the foreign office). He also managed to establish the Romanov dynasty, which would rule over Russia for the next few centuries. Michael I died in 1645, and his son, Alexis, succeeded him.

Michael I Romanov.
https://commons.wikimedia.org/wiki/File:Michael-I-Romanov-Wedekind.jpg

Alexis I had to deal with several riots in prominent cities like Novgorod and Pskov. During his reign, he also engaged in wars against Sweden and Poland. Despite all the trouble, he was known for being a peaceful ruler. He managed to enact a new legal code (the Sobornoye Ulozheniye), which led to the creation of a serf class and made official state documentation necessary to travel within the country. During this time, the Orthodox Church created new customs under the Great Moscow Synod, which led to the division of the church between those who adhered to the new traditions and the people who clung to the old traditions. Alexis I died in 1676 after about three decades of being on the throne.

Dynastic Dispute

Unfortunately, Alexis I's death caused another dynastic dispute, which would have consequences for the entire kingdom. The dispute began when the children of Alexis I's first wife and second wife began fighting over who had the right to the throne. At first, the fight was between Feodor III, Sofia Alekseyevna, and Ivan V, who were Alexis I's children from his first marriage, and Peter Alekseyevich, who was the son of Alexis I's second wife. Feodor III became the tsar but died after six years of ruling due to illness.

Ultimately, Ivan V and Peter were forced to share the Russian throne, an arrangement that would last until 1696, when Ivan V died.

Peter the Great

Peter Alekseyevich was born in 1672 to Alexis I and Natalya Kirillovna Naryshkina. When he inherited the throne in 1696 (after ruling beside his half-brother), he found that Russia was severely underdeveloped compared to other European countries. Russia was mostly cut off from the Western world and had rejected any attempts to connect with the West, which meant Russia was cut off from modern movements like the Renaissance and Reformation. Peter wanted more for Russia and almost immediately instituted massive reforms to modernize the country. He reorganized the Russian army, involved himself in the Russian Orthodox Church, reorganized the territorial divisions of the country, and separated schools from religious control.

Peter the Great.
Jean-Marc Nattier, Public domain, via Wikimedia Commons;
https://commons.wikimedia.org/wiki/File:Jean-Marc_Nattier,_Pierre_Ier_(1717)_-002.jpg

Unfortunately, Peter faced a lot of opposition from the nobility, as his reforms touched on every aspect of Russian life. He was able to move past the opposition and brought experts to Russia to advance technology. Peter founded the first Russian newspaper, refined the gentry, and updated the alphabet. He proved that he was a progressive thinker and worked hard to turn Russia into a great nation.

Peter was also a capable politician who appointed a senate, regulated state administration, and made great strides in foreign policy. He managed to gain more territories in Latvia, Finland, and Estonia and even defeated the Swedish Army in 1709. During the battle with the Swedish Army, Peter proved his military capabilities when he routed the Swedish troops to the city of Poltava during an especially brutal winter. Peter managed to secure access to the Black Sea after several wars with Turkey. He also commissioned the city of St. Petersburg along the Neva River, which would eventually be called the "window to Europe" and Russia's capital.

During his reign, he visited England to learn more about shipbuilding and navigation, which helped him build Russia's navy. King William III of England assisted Peter, as he was hoping for a way to increase trade with Russia. In 1703, Peter achieved his goal when a fleet was established in the Baltic Sea, allowing Russia to become a formidable naval power.

Peter the Great encouraged industrial growth, allowing the economy to flourish, and introduced many progressive policies that ushered Russia into a new age and brought it up to speed with European advancements.

Russo-Persian War

The Russo-Persian War is also known as Peter the Great's Persian campaign. Peter wanted to prevent the Ottoman Empire from taking land in the Caucasus and Caspian regions as Safavid Iran weakened. For years, Peter had been reforming his army and introducing new technologies to the Russian people. He also built a modern navy, something Russia had never had before.

It became clear that Peter's reforms had been successful since he secured a victory over Safavid Iran. The victory gave Russia control of areas in the North and South Caucasus, including the cities of Baku and Derbent. Russia also received the provinces of Gilan, Shirvan, Astarabad, and Mazandaran, as outlined in the Treaty of St. Petersburg.

Russia continued to control the Iranian territories for about a decade. However, during the Treaty of Resht of 1732 and the Treaty of Ganja of 1735, the lands were given back to Iran. Even though the lands were eventually returned to Iran, the Russo-Persian War was one of Peter the Great's last achievements and likely a source of great pride for the aging monarch since he personally participated in the campaigns.

Thanks to Peter the Great's victories, he was able to gain territories around the Baltic Sea, bringing an end to Swedish control of the Baltic. Peter the Great's reforms, foreign policies, and successful wars turned Russia into one of the most formidable European powers.

Tsar Peter the Great's Legacy

Peter the Great inherited a struggling nation that was completely behind its European peers. He sought to modernize Russia and turn it into one of the greatest nations on earth. For the most part, he was able to achieve his goals and earned his title of Peter the Great. While he had many achievements, his reign was not without its problems. Like many of his predecessors, he was known for being a tyrant who imposed cruel punishments on those who wronged him. His various reforms often led to an increase in taxes, but any rebellions or riots were immediately repressed.

Peter married twice and fathered about eleven legitimate children. Unfortunately, many of his children didn't survive infancy. He was a tall and handsome man who indulged in excessive tendencies and could be quite violent. While his reign was full of impressive achievements, he had a difficult personal life. His eldest son, Alexei, was found guilty of treason. Peter sentenced his son to death but sought any information that could exonerate him, even if the means of extracting that information meant torture. Alexei died after being interrogated in 1718.

Peter the Great died in 1725 and was entombed in St. Petersburg. He has been called the greatest Russian ruler, and his efforts certainly turned Russia into one of the great European nations. His efforts weren't always well received, and he often had to overcome formidable opposition from his own people as he reformed most parts of Russian life. Russia would be forever changed, and Peter the Great's legacy continues to be a source of pride for the Russian people.

Chapter 4: Catherine the Great and 18ᵗʰ-Century Russia

During the 18ᵗʰ century, Russia went through numerous major changes. Peter the Great built Russia's formidable navy and modernized the entire country. Once he died, his legacy would be continued by an unlikely source: a foreign woman. Catherine the Great rose to prominence during the 18ᵗʰ century and had a lasting impact on imperial Russia. She started off as a young princess in a strange court who eventually overthrew her own husband and took control of the country.

At this time, Russian explorers were making expeditions into the great unknown in the north while the Russian Enlightenment spread steadily throughout the vast country. The Russian Empire had been increasingly growing for years, but in the 18ᵗʰ century, it would finally reach its peak when it administered over five million square miles.

The Issue of Succession

Peter the Great was an excellent monarch who had many achievements. Unfortunately, he failed in one of the most vital aspects of his duties. He failed to name an heir before his death. His family life was somewhat complicated. Peter the Great was first married to Eudoxia Lopukhina, the daughter of a minor Russian noble, in 1689. However, the marriage wasn't a happy one, and he divorced Eudoxia in 1698. The couple had three children together, but only one survived childhood: the Tsarevich of Russia, Alexei

Petrovich. Peter the Great then married his mistress, Marta Helena Skowrońska, a Polish-Lithuanian peasant who converted to Russian Orthodoxy and changed her name to Catherine. The couple had several children, but few survived childhood.

Peter was greatly disappointed by the young tsarevich, who didn't share his imposing stature and propensity for war. In 1715, Peter the Great threatened to cut Alexei from the line of succession. The threat worked better than Peter had expected, as Alexei offered to relinquish his right to the throne. Alexei didn't share many of Peter's progressive ideas, and there was a good chance that once Peter died, Alexei would undo much of his father's work. Peter retaliated by ordering his son to either become a monk or a worthy successor. There were concerns that Alexei would draw Peter's enemies to his side and become a serious threat. Alexei agreed to become a monk but fled the country with his mistress and sought refuge in Austria.

Alexei was forced to return to Russia in 1718, where he was put on trial for treason. His father publicly disowned him. Alexei was imprisoned and brutally tortured. While under torture, Alexei admitted to plotting his father's demise. Peter oversaw the torture but hesitated to execute his son. Alexei died in prison. Eudoxia was also punished on the false charge of adultery and publicly flogged. She was then confined in a monastery. In 1724, Peter crowned his second wife as empress, but by then, all his male children were dead.

Struggle for Power

When Peter the Great died in 1725, his failure to name an heir became extremely serious since the Russian people wondered who to look to for leadership. Russian law dictated that the monarch had the right to name his heir, which meant that his next of kin wasn't automatically eligible for the throne. As soon as Peter died, his wife, Catherine I, took the throne, but she became a puppet for Peter's ministers. Peter's chief advisor, Prince Aleksandr Danilovich Menshikov, made most of the pertinent decisions in the empire, but the other nobles soon caught wind of what he was doing and forced him to share power with others.

Once Catherine I died, the nobles made Peter's grandson, Peter II, the new tsar in 1727. He was very young when he took the throne; he was only around eleven years old. Peter II was Tsarevich Alexei's son through his marriage to a German princess. Nobles vied for power, and Peter II was used as a pawn. Menshikov aimed to marry the young tsar to his sixteen-year-old daughter Maria. However, Menshikov became sick, and Peter II was quickly influenced by other nobles who convinced the young tsar to exile Menshikov. Peter II complied but died in 1730.

The throne went to Peter the Great's niece, Anna. Anna's rule supported the old ways of doing things, undoing some of the progress made by Peter I, especially in regard to how the nobles were treated. She attempted to put her heir on the throne but was thwarted by the nobles who supported Peter I's daughter, Elizabeth. She gladly took the throne and continued many of her father's reforms.

Elizabeth I of Russia.
https://commons.wikimedia.org/wiki/File:Elizabeth_of_Russia_by_anonim_after_Caravaq ue_(18_c,_priv.coll).jpg

Elizabeth I was a capable ruler who opened Russia's first university and won several notable battles. However, Elizabeth remained childless. Unlike her father, Elizabeth took care to name her heir. She chose her nephew, Peter, to succeed her and arranged his marriage to Princess Sophie of Anhalt-Zerbst. Elizabeth died in 1762.

The Great Northern Expedition

The Great Northern Expedition was one of the greatest exploration efforts in history. It was initiated by Peter the Great, who commissioned Vitus Bering to explore the Asian Pacific coast. The first and second expeditions resulted in the mapping of most of Siberia and some parts of North America, which had previously been unknown. The First Kamchatka Expedition lasted from 1725 to 1731, while the Second Kamchatka Expedition lasted from 1733 to 1743. The Second Kamchatka Expedition was incredibly successful and was later called the Great Northern Expedition.

Originally, Peter the Great wanted to find a North Sea route from Europe to the Pacific for the Russian Navy. The expedition was funded by the Admiralty College in St. Petersburg, and over three thousand people were involved. It was one of the largest projects of its kind in history.

Russia's discoveries (Map published by the Imperial Academy of St. Petersburg).
https://commons.wikimedia.org/wiki/File;Jefferys_-_The_Russian_Discoveries.jpg#file

The expedition led to the discovery of Alaska, the Commander Islands, Bering Island, and the Aleutian Islands. It also resulted in detailed cartographical information of the northern coast of the Kuril Islands and Russia. For years, it was believed there was another landmass in the North Pacific, but this expedition helped to clear up that myth. It also resulted in extensive scientific research on Kamchatka and Siberia. Unfortunately, the expedition failed to find the Northeast Passage.

The Great Northern Expedition was a product of the Russian Enlightenment, and while it was one of Peter I's dreams, Empress Anna and Elizabeth I made the expedition a reality.

Peter III

Peter was born in the Duchy of Holstein-Gottorp to the duke of Holstein-Gottorp, Charles, and Anna Petrovna, the daughter of Peter the Great. Unfortunately, his mother died when he was still an infant, and his father died a few years later, leaving the young boy an orphan. His aunt, Elizabeth I, called him to Russia in 1742, where she proclaimed him as her heir. Elizabeth I also arranged his marriage to his second cousin. Sophia converted to the Russian Orthodox Church and changed her name to Catherine. However, their marriage was extremely unhappy. Reports indicate that Peter was an abrasive young man who made Catherine's life difficult. It should be noted that most of the information about Peter is derived from Catherine's memoirs.

Peter III and Catherine II of Russia.
https://commons.wikimedia.org/wiki/File:Peter_III_and_Catherine_II_of_Russia_(Anna_Rosina_Lisiewska)_-_Nationalmuseum_-_15939.tif

When Elizabeth I died, Peter took the throne, but he wasn't popular with the Russian people, who viewed him as a foreign ruler. Peter might have been Russian, but he was born in Germany and barely spoke any Russian. He also endorsed foreign policies and thinking. Peter was a pro-Prussian ruler who withdrew troops from the Seven Years' War. He also planned to go to war against Denmark but was overthrown before he could.

Peter showed a profound lack of understanding of his own country, as he endorsed the Lutheran religion. While this may have been an attempt to introduce religious freedom, his decisions were viewed as anti-Orthodox, which alienated him from his subjects. Peter and Catherine had one son together named Paul.

The Seven Years' War

The Seven Years' War has been called the first real "world war," as it involved an alliance of Russia, France, Sweden, Austria, and Saxony against Hanover, Great Britain, and Prussia. The war took place between 1756 and 1763. It took on an international component, as Britain and France fought against each other in India and North America.

The war can be traced back to 1748. The War of the Austrian Succession ended with the Treaty of Aix-la-Chapelle, which many viewed as a temporary measure. Austria lost the region of Silesia to Prussia, which was a wealthy land. Tensions brewed between the two countries, and their allies began preparing for war. Russia was worried about the increasing strength of Prussia and was willing to become allies with Austria to stop them.

In 1756, Frederick II of Prussia attacked Saxony, breaking its alliance with Austria. Eventually, Austria's allies attacked Prussia from all sides. The Prussians were forced to retreat in the face of the Franco-Russo-Austrian alliance. While the Prussians won a few battles, they needed something to change. Elizabeth I was notoriously anti-Prussian, but her successor, Peter III, didn't have the same views. Eventually, Russia entered into negotiations, and by 1763, most of Europe was feeling the financial strain of fighting the war. In 1763, the Treaty of Paris was signed, settling many issues between Britain, France, and Spain. The war led to the increased prestige of Prussia and Russia, while Spain and Holland were greatly reduced.

Rise of Catherine the Great

In 1762, Peter had been ruling for six months and had vastly underestimated his wife's hatred. During this time, he took a holiday to Oranienbaum while Catherine was left in St. Petersburg. She arranged a military regiment to protect her from Peter, and the clergy ordained her as the Russian ruler. She then arrested Peter and forced him to abdicate. Peter was assassinated a few days later by Alexei Orlov. While the timing of his death is suspicious, there is no evidence that Catherine murdered her husband.

Catherine the Great.
https://commons.wikimedia.org/wiki/File:Catherine_II_by_F.Rokotov_after_Roslin_(1780 s,_Hermitage).jpg)

Peter had proven that he didn't understand his own people, but Catherine was not like her husband. Catherine learned Russian almost as soon as she arrived in Russia and even spoke with a Russian accent while her husband could barely speak the language. During her marriage to Peter, she had taken the time to ingratiate herself with many powerful figures in the court. Once she sat on the throne, she quickly focused on expanding Russia's borders and continued many of Peter the Great's reforms. Catherine added the territories of Belarus, Lithuania, and Crimea to Russia. After making arrangements with Prussia and Austria, she received many lands in Central Europe.

Catherine instituted financial reforms and worked hard to improve Russia's economy. She was intensely interested in public health and opened several hospitals. The army was forced to update its medical practices under her reign. She even had herself inoculated against smallpox, which was a controversial procedure at the time. When the procedure worked, she promoted inoculations throughout the empire. Catherine's husband had ruled for about six months, but Catherine would go on to rule for over three decades and earn the title of "Catherine the Great."

Notable Features of the Catherinian Era

One of Catherine's goals was to incorporate Russia's culture and economy into Europe. She was an avid reader of philosophical books and particularly enjoyed the works of Diderot and Voltaire. In her opinion, Russia needed to catch up to Europe. She gave the press creative freedom, managed the economy well, and opened spaces where learned people could meet. All of these factors contributed to the Russian Enlightenment and intellectual life.

Catherine was responsible for a number of progressive reforms, including the Statute on the Provinces of 1775, which aimed to improve the government and institute more orphanages, schools, and hospitals. She set rules for provincial and municipal services and encouraged the nobles to take better care of their serfs. In Russia, serfs were people owned by noble landowners. They gave away their rights in exchange for protection and support during difficult times. They worked on the nobles' lands and were required to pay a portion of their grain as taxes to the nobles. Serfs had limited rights, but Catherine afforded them new rights. For example, if a noble wasn't taking care of their serfs, the serfs were allowed to make a complaint. This gave serfs bureaucratic status they previously didn't have. Serfs also became more educated, as some nobles chose to send certain serfs to schools opened by Catherine. They would return as skilled employees whom the nobles employed.

Catherine stimulated the economy by lowering grain prices to increase exports and decreased the regulation of manufacturing. Her reforms brought about a golden age in Russian history, which would survive after her death in 1796.

The Russian Enlightenment

Catherine the Great considered herself to be one of Europe's most enlightened rulers, and many historians are inclined to believe this claim. The Russian Enlightenment was inspired by ideas pioneered in Western Europe. It first found prominence under Peter the Great but reached a new high under Catherine the Great. The Enlightenment was a period of cultural change that brought about developments in fields like architecture, mathematics, and fashion. Enlightenment ideals were centered around innovation, the search for knowledge, and progress. Russian leaders held absolute power and used this to either encourage or hinder the Russian Enlightenment.

St. Petersburg quickly became the capital of the Russian Enlightenment, and the movement reached the nobles first. Children of nobles were sent to Western European schools, where they learned about mathematics, science, and literature. The Enlightenment also helped modernize the Russian army, as Peter the Great's reforms aimed to greatly improve the army according to Western European standards. Peter the Great was so eager to modernize Russia that he imposed a beard tax on Russians, forcing them to shave to look more like Western Europeans. Beards had traditionally been a sign of manliness in Russian culture, but that didn't matter in Peter the Great's quest to modernize the country. Soon, the noble court began wearing Western European fashions, especially French fashion.

Catherine the Great continued Peter the Great's efforts to modernize Russia. Her efforts led to Russia's golden age.

The Peasant Uprising of 1773

In 1773, Yemelyan Pugachev led what would become one of the most influential rebellions in Russian history. While Catherine the Great brought about reforms that benefited the serfs, most didn't feel the benefits. To secure the nobles' cooperation, she increased the nobles' authority over the serfs, which led to increasing unrest. Between 1762 and 1769, more than fifty rebellions broke out. Unrest grew to a fevered pitch.

Pugachev gained support from the peasants and Cossacks because he promised to secure more rights for the serfs, including lands of their own. In the past, serfs could appeal to the monarch if they were abused by nobles, but Catherine the Great cut off this communication when she decreed that serfs could make formal complaints with the government instead. This angered many serfs. Pugachev was able to rally thousands of rebels until he led an army of about 100,000.

At the time, Russia was locked in a war against Turkey. However, Catherine the Great was forced to resolve that quickly in order to have enough troops to bring an end to the rebellions.

The Cossacks were known for being skilled and brutal warriors who were obligated to help the Russian army. Pugachev was a Cossack who ended up defecting from the army. The Russian government alienated numerous Cossacks when they revoked many of the Cossacks' privileges, which caused many Cossacks to join Pugachev's cause.

Pugachev took on the name of Peter III and issued a manifesto that gave serfs freedom and the right to own their land. The rebellion dragged on for over a year and spread like wildfire. Rebels were encouraged to kill nobles, and it is estimated that hundreds of nobles were murdered. The government killed thousands of rebels, while others were branded and sent to Siberian prisons.

The rebellion was finally suppressed in 1774, and Pugachev was executed. However, Pugachev's rebellion inspired new ideas in the minds of serfs, and imperial Russia was impacted by the echoes of the rebellion until its fall in 1917.

The Russian Army in the 18th Century

During the 18th century, the Russian army experienced a "golden age." Thanks to Peter the Great's efforts, the Russian army became one of the best forces in the world, as it managed to defeat Poland, Sweden, and the Ottoman Empire. The army and navy were highly organized, and progressive reforms gave Russian soldiers access to new technologies and tactics. At the time, the Imperial Russian Army was a prestigious institution that was only surpassed by the church and the royals. Most social classes were involved in the army in one way or another.

Badge of the Russian Imperial Army.

Peter the Great introduced conscription in 1699. Peasants were conscripted according to population numbers, and in the 18th century, conscription was for life. At first, commoners were able to rise through the ranks of the army and were given titles. However, this practice was abolished during Catherine the Great's reign. A notable general from this period was Alexander Suvorov, who fought in Crimea and the Caucasus. He also fought during the Russo-Turkish War, which lasted from 1787 to 1792. He won many victories for the Russian army and was highly decorated.

The Imperial Russian Army was a formidable power that would serve Russia well when Napoleon decided to invade.

Chapter 5: From Napoleon to the Crimean War

The 18ᵗʰ century ushered in a golden age in Russian history, with progressive leaders introducing reforms that modernized the army and stimulated the economy. This meant Russia was in a good position in the years leading up to Napoleon's invasion. The 19ᵗʰ century brought more changes, and Russian monarchs strived to live up to the legacy of their predecessors. It was a time marked by revolts and opposing ideas that would eventually lead to the end of the Russian golden age.

In time, Russia would become embroiled in the Crimean War, a grueling military engagement that would have disastrous consequences for the Imperial Russian Army.

Napoleon's Invasion of Russia

In 1799, Napoleon Bonaparte took power in France and became a serious threat to Europe. He took Belgium, Holland, parts of Italy, Germany, and Croatia. It seemed the French emperor was invincible, as his power grew to include parts of Poland, Spain, and Switzerland. No one seemed to be able to beat Napoleon.

At the time, the Russians were experiencing the negative impacts of Napoleon's reign since trade declined sharply. Tsar Alexander I, who ruled Russia at the time, decided to push back against Napoleon by enforcing a strict tax on French products and refused to give one of his sisters to Napoleon in marriage. Russia was also trading with Britain, the latter of which was one of France's biggest rivals.

Napoleon wanted to teach Alexander I a lesson and amassed a massive army to invade Russia in June 1812. He had every reason to be confident, as his Grande Armèe numbered around 450,000, while the Russian army numbered around 200,000. Napoleon expected to defeat the Russians quickly and force Alexander I into negotiations.

The Russians had another plan. The Grande Armèe captured the city of Vilna a few days after the initial invasion, and to their surprise, the Russians put up very little fight. As Napoleon advanced, the Russians pulled back into the interior. To make matters worse, Russian roads were in a deplorable state, making it impossible for supply carts to reach the French army in time. Winter was setting in, and thousands of French soldiers and horses died from exposure. As the Russians retreated, they set fire to fields and supplies that could aid the French. The Russians employed a scorched-earth policy, which caused the French to become increasingly desperate. Soon, the French soldiers were afflicted with diseases like typhus and dysentery, which decimated their ranks.

Finally, in September 1812, the Russians made a stand, leading to the Battle of Borodino, which led to significant losses on both sides. When the Grande Armèe entered Moscow a few days later, they found the Russians had set fire to the historic city. There were large amounts of liquor left behind but no food. Napoleon was forced to retreat soon after due to the winter. It had become apparent the Grande Armèe couldn't maintain its position.

The Grande Armèe was pressed for food and supplies. The massive army's numbers had dwindled down to about 100,000 men. The Russian army constantly attacked the Grande Armèe's rearguard, which led to even more casualties. As winter progressed, thousands more died from the cold. Reports state that some men cut open dead animals and crawled inside for warmth, while others say soldiers stacked dead bodies over windows and doors to keep the cold out.

By December, Napoleon had to return to Paris, as rumors of a coup reached him. It took a few more days for the French to leave

Russia completely. The disastrous invasion was the beginning of the end for Napoleon.

The Defeat of Napoleon

The invasion of Russia left Napoleon in a weakened state, and Prussia, Sweden, and Austria decided to help Britain and Russia defeat Napoleon once and for all. Napoleon quickly assembled a new army. While it was almost as large as his previous army, the soldiers lacked battle experience. In October 1813, he suffered a massive defeat at the Battle of Leipzig. A few months later, Paris was captured, and Napoleon was exiled to Elba.

However, Napoleon was far from ready to give up. He was able to escape Elba in 1815 and immediately returned to France, where he set up his government. Allied troops quickly responded to his escape, but Napoleon won significant victories against the Prussians. His goal was to prevent Europe from uniting. In June, Napoleon led his troops to meet Arthur Wellesley, Duke of Wellington, at the village of Waterloo in Brussels. Napoleon made a series of fatal mistakes, and the Duke of Wellington proved to be a formidable enemy. The French army was defeated, and Napoleon was forced to retreat. He later abdicated in favor of his son and surrendered to the British. Napoleon was exiled to the remote island of St. Helena, where he died a few years later of stomach cancer.

The Decembrist Revolt of 1825

Tsar Alexander I died unexpectedly on December 1st, 1825, and his royal guards quickly rallied around his brother, Constantine Pavlovich. However, Constantine had renounced his rights to the throne, so Alexander I's younger brother, Nicholas, decided to take the throne for himself.

Meanwhile, some imperial officers decided to create a society known as the Union of Salvation in 1816. In 1825, the society split into Southern and Northern factions. The Northern Society wanted a constitutional monarchy, equality in the law, and the abolishment of serfdom. The Southern Society was more radical and wanted to create a republic that redistributed lands between the state and the peasants, as well as abolish the monarchy. Many officers belonging to the Union of Salvation were indignant about the injustices faced by peasants and rejected courtly traditions, instead preferring an academic lifestyle. They embraced the "Russian way of life" that the peasants experienced.

The Northern Society refused to support the new tsar. Instead, they proclaimed their support of Constantine. On December 26th, 1825, about three thousand rebels showed up at Senate Square. They were faced with nine thousand loyal troops. Nicholas I chose to send a war hero, Count Mikhail Miloradovich, to negotiate with the rebels, but he was shot during his speech.

The rebels attempted to take the Winter Palace but were forced to retreat. Nicholas I ordered a cavalry charge on the rebels but was forced to retreat as well. He then ordered his troops to open fire on the rebels, who retreated and tried to regroup on the frozen waters of the Neva River. Nicholas's troops shot cannons at the ice, which caused many rebels to fall into the icy waters. With so many rebel deaths, the revolt came to an end, and the remaining rebels were exiled to Siberia.

The Decembrists failed in their attempts but created a divide between the government and reformers, which would only become bigger and eventually lead to more revolutionary movements.

Nicholas I

Nicholas I was deeply impacted by the Decembrist movement since he could have been killed. As a result, he abandoned many of the progressive reforms initiated by his predecessors and focused on Russian nationalism, autocracy, and the Russian Orthodox Church. It also caused him to become determined to control Russian society and solidified his belief that he needed to be an autocrat who did whatever was necessary to restrain the people.

The government started censoring many areas of public life, such as education and publications. One of Nicholas I's ministers introduced "autocracy, Orthodoxy, and nationality" as the main principles of the government. The Third Section of His Imperial Chancellery (the secret police) was equipped with spies and informers, who were spread throughout the country.

Nicholas I of Russia.

The tsar's unlimited power was emphasized, and the traditions of Russian Orthodoxy became increasingly emphasized. However, these policies led to the repression of the Russian people, foreigners, and non-Russian religions. He also became more aggressive toward the Ottoman Empire. Nicholas I left behind a legacy of being one of the most reactionary leaders in European history.

The Russo-Persian War (1826–1828)

The Russians and Persians had long fought over territories located along the Caspian Sea and in the Transcaucasus. Two Russo-Persian wars had already taken place; the first lasted from 1804 to 1813, while the second occurred between 1826 and 1828. The Persian Shah Fath-Ali hoped to claim Karabakh, Talesh, Shakki, and Shirvan, as he wanted to prevent the Russians from taking over the territories when they annexed the Kingdom of Georgia (which had also been claimed by the Persians). Meanwhile, the Russians wanted to capture more territories, especially along the Kura and Aras Rivers. The First Russo-Persian War was won by the Russians, who were able to obtain a lot of the territories they were after, including northern Azerbaijan and

Dagestan, turning the local territories into vassal states.

Soon after Alexander I died, the Persians decided to invade Russian territories while the Russian government was dealing with the Decembrist Revolt. At first, the Persians managed to secure several victories while the Russian general, Alexei Yermolov, desperately tried to secure reinforcements from St. Petersburg. While the Russians were caught unaware, they were able to prevent the Persians from advancing too far. In 1827, the Russians captured several Persian territories, including Yerevan and Tabriz. The Persians were forced to abandon their war efforts and signed the Treaty of Turkmenchay in 1828, which allowed the Russians to keep Yerevan and the territories leading up to the Aras River. The Persians were also forced to pay about twenty million rubles to the Russians.

Greek Revolution of 1821

Greece had been ruled by the Ottomans since the 15th century. For years, the Greeks tried to overthrow the Ottomans but remained unsuccessful until 1821. In 1814, a secret society called the Society of Friends was formed due to the revolutionary ideas sweeping through Europe. Their aim was to liberate Greece and finally overthrow the Turks. In 1821, a widespread revolution broke out, which the Ottomans struggled to put down. However, the Greeks soon began fighting between themselves, and the Turks called on their vassal states for help, including the Eyalet of Egypt (a part of Egypt controlled by the Ottomans). The revolution began failing as the Turks began winning more territories.

However, Britain, France, and Russia decided to get involved. At the Battle of Navarino in 1827, the Ottoman-Egyptian fleet was destroyed. Russia invaded the Ottoman Empire, and the Turks were forced to grant the Greeks their freedom in the Treaty of Adrianople in 1829.

The Russo-Turkish War (1828–1829)

The Turks didn't take Russian involvement in the Greek Revolution lightly. In retaliation for the Battle of Navarino, the Ottoman sultan, Mahmud II, closed the Dardanelles (an internationally significant waterway in Turkey) to Russian ships, which left both sides poised for war. In the beginning, Emperor Nicholas I commanded the Russian army, while Agha Hussein Pasha led the Ottoman army. The fighting started in the Balkans, namely in modern-day Bulgaria, against three important Ottoman strongholds: Varna, Silistra, and Shumen. The fighting was intense. The Russians took Varna but were forced to retreat due to their ill-equipped soldiers and the diseases that were raging through the ranks. The Russians managed to capture Burgas and Adrianople, which were heavy blows for the Ottoman Empire.

Besides fighting in the Balkans, fighting also took place in the Caucasus. The Russian army was able to win several territories on this front. During the war, thousands of Armenians were forced to move into Russian territory.

Eventually, the Ottoman sultan was forced to negotiate a peace treaty since he faced such a significant loss of territory. On September 14th, 1829, the Treaty of Adrianople was signed. Russia obtained territories east of the Black Sea and the mouth of the Danube. The sultan also gave Russia control of parts of Armenia, and it was allowed to occupy Wallachia and Moldavia. The treaty forced the sultan to recognize Greek independence.

The Russo-Turkish War led to significant territorial gains for the Russian Empire and helped the Greeks finally bring an end to their nearly decade-long war for freedom.

The Polish Uprising (1830–1831)

The Polish Uprising, or November Uprising, saw armed Polish troops rise up against Russia. In 1795, Poland was no longer an autonomous political entity. In 1807, the Duchy of Warsaw was created as a result of Poland's participation in the Napoleonic Wars. When Napoleon was defeated, Poland was divided between Austria, which received territories in the south; Russia, which received hegemony over the Congress Kingdom of Poland; and Prussia, which took control of the Grand Duchy of Poznan. The Congress Kingdom had its own constitution and was only supposed to be indirectly subject to Russia. However, the Russian monarchy frequently disregarded the constitution.

In 1829, Nicholas I claimed the title of "King of Poland." Grand Duke Constantine (the one who didn't want the throne) was the governor of Poland. He disregarded the Polish constitution and abolished several Polish patriotic societies. Constantine replaced Polish administrators with Russians and allowed serious conflicts to develop within the Polish army. To make matters worse, the Russians planned to use the Polish army to bring an end to the Belgian Revolution and France's July Revolution.

A group of Polish rebels took up arms in 1830 and attacked Constantine's seat of power at Belweder Palace. They managed to take the city's arsenal, and the local Polish government was quickly reorganized. The Polish hoped to gain their complete freedom but soon faced an all-out war against Russia. While the Polish fought hard and found many sympathetic voices, the major powers of the time—Britain and France—didn't come to their aid. In October 1831, the remainder of the Polish army surrendered to Russia.

After the uprising ended, Polish women wore black jewelry to profess their mourning for the loss of their homeland.

Slavophiles vs. Westernizers

Peter the Great implemented several reforms with the hopes of replacing traditionalist and medieval systems with the principles of the Enlightenment. Some of Peter the Great's predecessors, especially Catherine the Great, endorsed his reforms and imposed more changes to Russian politics, economics, education, and culture. Machinery was modernized, the bureaucracy was refined, and Western European tastes and ideals were upheld. This led to the development of a group called the Westernizers, who emphatically believed Russia needed to adhere to Western European values and ideas.

Not everyone was happy about the Westernization of Russia, though. Slavophilia was a movement that opposed the values of Western Europe. They didn't want Russia to embrace democracy, materialism, or atheism; instead, they promoted the values of medieval Russia. Some admitted a few Western values had merit, while others rejected all Western ideas and promoted the absolute power of the tsar and the church. The Slavophiles believed they were protecting Russia's culture and traditions. Rural life was glorified, and Slavophiles endeavored to protect peasant communities against the growing working class. Many Slavophiles adopted traditional Russian aesthetics and rejected Peter the Great's reforms. The Slavophiles also endorsed a militant stance of religious intolerance.

While the 18th century saw the rise of the Russian Enlightenment, the 19th century saw the rejection of many of those ideals, especially under the reign of Nicholas I, whose government upheld many Slavophile ideals.

The Crimean War (1853–1856)

By the 1850s, the Ottoman Empire was in a massive decline, and Nicholas I saw the opportunity to expand Russia's borders. However, Britain and France were concerned a Russian takeover would negatively impact their trade routes and were determined to prevent Nicholas I's power grab. The Crimean War took place in the Crimean Peninsula and was the conflict that made Florence Nightingale, the founder of modern nursing, famous. It was a brutal war that caused the deaths of about 650,000 people.

The Attack on the Malakoff (the main Russian fortification before Sevastopol during the Crimean War).

Tensions rose between Orthodox worshipers and Catholics who wanted access to holy sites ruled by the Turks. After several Orthodox monks were killed in Bethlehem, Nicholas I demanded that the Orthodox worshipers be allowed to access religious sites freely and that he should be made the protector of Orthodox worshipers in the Ottoman Empire. The Turks refused, and Nicholas invaded the Turkish principalities of Walachia and Moldavia. The Turks declared war on Russia in 1853.

The Russians slaughtered thousands of Ottoman soldiers and sailors. The brutality of the war inflamed Europe to fight Russia.

Britain and France joined Turkey and sent their armies and navies to protect the Middle Eastern nation, especially Istanbul. The British and French expected a short engagement but soon found themselves embroiled in a bloody war that dragged on.

Both sides suffered heavy casualties, and the Russian Imperial Army found itself besieged from all sides. When Austria threatened to join the fight against Russia, the Russians were forced to end the war and signed the Treaty of Paris in March 1856. The Russians had to give up the territories they had seized, and their army was never the same again. Tensions between the Turks and Russians continued for years. They even found themselves on opposite sides in World War I.

Chapter 6: Tsar Alexander II's Reforms and Tsar Alexander III's Setback to Autocracy

The Crimean War was a brutal conflict that led to the deaths of thousands of Russian soldiers. It severely diminished the Russian army, which had been a formidable force for decades. When Tsar Alexander II took the throne, he instituted a number of radical reforms that could have changed Russia forever. However, his reforms angered powerful people, and he was assassinated in the streets of St. Petersburg.

His successor, Alexander III, didn't have the same goals of reformation as his father, so Alexander II's reforms were promptly reversed. Alexander III faced many challenges while firmly establishing his autocratic rule but boasted a few notable achievements, such as the construction of the Trans-Siberian Railway.

Tsar Alexander II

Alexander II was born in 1818 and was the oldest son of Tsar Nicholas I and Charlotte of Prussia. During his early years, St. Petersburg was far from the intellectual center that it had once been. Any intellectual innovation or freedom of thought was strongly suppressed, and speaking against the government was a serious offense. Unlike his father, Alexander II wasn't interested in war and shared many of the same notions as his teacher, the liberal poet Vasily Zhukovsky. He was reported to be a kind and gentle young man.

Alexander II of Russia.
Nikolay Lavrov, Public domain, via Wikimedia Commons;
https://commons.wikimedia.org/wiki/File:Alexander_II_of_Russia_by_N.Lavrov_(1868,_Museum_of_Artillery).jpg

Alexander II's father died in 1855, and he ascended to the throne. For the first few months of his reign, he was preoccupied with settling the Crimean War, which had become a costly and humiliating drain on Russia's resources. As soon as the war was concluded, he began enacting a number of reforms. Many of the educated classes supported Alexander II's reforms since they were eager to develop Russia's natural resources and reorganize the government's administration.

Alexander II proved to be a shrewd and cautious man who used his autocracy to bring about practical and progressive reforms. However, not everyone was happy with his reforms, and he became the target of a number of assassination attempts.

Some of his reforms included reorganizing the navy and army. He followed the French model to create a new judicial administration system and penal code. Alexander II simplified the criminal and civil processes, found a way for rural districts to govern themselves with elective assemblies, and abolished capital punishment.

Serf Emancipation of 1861

Alexander II made some changes to the legislation that allowed new freedoms in industry and commerce. As a result, a number of limited liability companies were created. He also wanted to construct a vast network of railways so intellectuals could more easily develop Russia's natural resources and increase the army's ability to protect the country. However, the more reforms he developed, the more he realized that serfdom was a serious problem. Alexander II created a number of committees dedicated to improving the serfs' situation. Emancipation committees were required to follow principles set by the monarch.

The question of solving the problems brought about by serfdom impacted all of Russian life, from the economy to politics. Alexander was presented with the problem of whether or not serfs should be laborers who were economically dependent on their landlords or if they should be allowed to become a class of landowners. Alexander II wanted the serfs to be able to own their own land, and on March 3rd, 1861, the serfs were emancipated.

Sale of Alaskan Territory to the US

For years, Russia had been looking to sell its territory in Alaska. The area was remote and extremely difficult to defend. Selling the territory made more sense than losing the land to Russian enemies. US President Andrew Johnson's secretary of state, William Seward, took the lead in discussions with Russia.

Negotiations for the sale began in March 1867, and while Seward was enthusiastic about the project, the American population didn't agree with his sentiments. Most believed the land was barren and useless. The project was called "Andrew Johnson's Polar Bear Garden" and "Seward's Folly." Much of the animosity may have resulted from Johnson's unpopular term as president.

Despite the unpopularity of the project, about 586,412 square miles of Alaskan territory was sold for $7.2 million, which amounted to a little less than 2 cents per acre.

Russo-Turkish War of 1877-1878

Even though the Crimean War ended and Russia had given back the territory it had taken during the war, there was still lingering animosity between Russia and the Ottoman Empire. In 1877, those tensions turned into an all-out war when the Russians and Turks disagreed over the rights of Orthodox Slavs who lived in the Balkans. The Treaty of Paris stated the Balkan Christians were to be protected by the European powers. When peasants rebelled in Bulgaria in 1876, the Turkish brutally put down the revolts.

This led to anti-Turkish efforts in Serbia. In 1876, several European powers met in Constantinople to come up with a compromise, which the Turks rejected in 1877. To protect the Balkan Slavs, Russia represented the European powers and prepared for war. The Russians launched an offensive in the Balkans and the Caucasus region. They were ultimately successful, and the war was concluded with the Treaty of San Stefano in 1878.

The Russians negotiated independence for Serbia, Romania, and Montenegro while receiving a large portion of Turkish territory for itself. Russia also pressed for the autonomy of Bulgaria, which would be ruled with Russian influence. However, Britain and Austria-Hungary forced Russia to revise the Treaty of San Stefano at the Congress of Berlin a few months later. The revisions angered many parties and caused tensions that would explode in the future.

While the Congress of Berlin allowed many Russian gains, it was still viewed as a defeat. Many Russians felt that Germany had failed to support Russia at the Congress of Berlin. Austria-Hungary was also seen with increasing suspicion, which had started during the Crimean War.

Alexander II's Assassination

Alexander II faced many assassination attempts. He was a progressive leader, but he retained his autocracy and was known for opposing political parties that opposed him, which earned him many enemies. In 1866, Dmitry Karakozov tried to kill the tsar. After Alexander II escaped death, he built a series of churches to commemorate his escape. In 1879, a former student named Alexander Soloviev attempted to shoot the tsar in the Square of the Guards Staff. The tsar had seen the revolver that Soloviev was carrying and ran away.

That same year, a radical group of revolutionists formed the Narodnaya Volya, or People's Will. The group aimed to create a social revolution and was willing to use terrorism to attain its goal. In 1880, some rebels placed a bomb under the dining room in the Winter Palace. Alexander II was late to dinner and narrowly missed the explosion, but sixty-seven other people were killed or injured.

In 1881, Alexander II signed the Loris-Melikov Constitution, which aimed to create legislative commissions comprised of elected officials. On the day he signed the proclamation, his carriage was traveling along the streets of St. Petersburg when a bomb went off, injuring surrounding civilians. Reports indicate that Alexander survived the initial blast but was met by a suicide bomber who hit him with a grenade. Tsar Alexander II died from his injuries a few hours later. All the assassins were executed. Alexander II's successor, Alexander III, rejected the Loris-Melikov Constitution.

Alexander III

Alexander III was born in 1845 and was the son of Alexander II and Maria of Hesse. Unlike his father, he didn't harbor liberal sentiments and was seen as unrefined and physically powerful. He was his father's second son, and he had little hope of inheriting the throne since his oldest brother, Nicholas, was healthy. Nicholas received the education of a prince, while Alexander was educated as a grand duke, which didn't go much further beyond secondary instruction. When Nicholas died suddenly in 1865, Alexander was thrust into the spotlight and had to study the principles of law and administration. It is believed that Alexander's teacher, Konstantin Pobedonostsev, inspired Alexander's belief that Russian Orthodoxy was a cornerstone of Russian patriotism. Alexander was married to Princess Dagmar of Denmark, who had previously been engaged to his brother Nicholas. Their marriage proved to be a happy one.

Alexander III of Russia.
Unknown photographer, CC BY-SA 4.0 <https://creativecommons.org/licenses/by-sa/4.0>,
via Wikimedia Commons;
https://commons.wikimedia.org/wiki/File:Tsar_Alexander_III_of_Russia_2.jpg

During the last years of Alexander II's reign, it became clear there was a divide between the monarch and his heir. Alexander II sometimes openly ridiculed Slavophiles, while his son was becoming more of a Slavophile by the day. Another notable difference between the two was that Alexander II had pro-German tendencies, while the tsarevich displayed pro-French sympathies.

When Alexander II was assassinated in 1881, Alexander III was finally able to enact his ideas. During his time as tsarevich, he uncovered rampant corruption within the government and wanted to reform the military. Alexander III also disapproved of many of his father's progressive reforms, believing the reforms had led to the problems Russia was facing. As a result, he reversed much of his father's work as soon as he became king.

The Famine of 1891/92

In 1891, a dry autumn prevented the Russian peasants from planting their fields on time. The delay would prove to be disastrous. The subsequent winter was unusually cold, but almost no snow fell. Snow was supposed to freeze the Volga River and protect seedlings from frost. Unfortunately, the Volga River flooded, and the frost killed the rest of the seedlings. The flood also destroyed fodder that was supposed to feed horses. The next spring was extremely windy, and it carried away topsoil and the remaining seedlings. Then, summer began early and proved to be long and dry. As a result, horses, peasants, and crops began to die. To make matters worse, there were several widespread cholera outbreaks.

The government blamed the famine on a poor harvest and prevented newspapers from reporting what was going on. There was more than enough grain to feed the dying peasants, but the railways weren't able to distribute the grain quickly enough. The government also delayed closing grain exports, and when they finally did, the merchants had a month's warning, which caused them to quickly export what they had. The minister of finance, Ivan Vyshnegradsky, shouldered a lot of the blame, as he had raised taxes so that peasants would sell more grain.

In late 1891, the government urged citizens to form anti-famine organizations. One of the volunteers who formed a committee was the famous writer Leo Tolstoy, who publicly blamed the Russian Orthodox Church and the tsar for mismanaging the situation. He was excommunicated for his criticisms, and the church forbade people from accepting his relief efforts.

Several royals, including the tsar and tsarina, raised a few million rubles for starving peasants. Local governments received about 150 million rubles in relief money, but they were only allowed to lend to peasants who would be able to pay them back. Many starving peasants were forced to eat raw flour and "famine bread," which was made from moss, bark, and husks. In 1892, the government bought about thirty thousand horses to plow the fields. The American government raised about $75 million (about $2 billion in modern currency) to help the Russians; the money was mainly given out in the form of loans.

The famine started along the Volga River and spread as far as the Black Sea and the Urals. By the time the famine came to an end, nearly half a million people had died. This caused lasting anger toward the tsarist government.

May Laws

The May Laws were a program of temporary laws enacted by Alexander III in May 1882 pertaining to the Jews in Russia. When Alexander II was assassinated, the blame was placed on the Russian

Jewish population. As a result, anti-Jewish sentiments rose, which led to a number of extremely violent riots. To make matters worse, the government declared the problem had risen because of Alexander II's reforms, which were significantly more progressive than Alexander III's own views.

To come up with a solution to the violence, Jewish representatives met with government officials in 1882. One of the proposed solutions was a mass exodus of the Jewish people from Russia to Central Asia. This was seen as an extreme measure, so a number of "temporary laws" were negotiated. The problem was the rural peasant class viewed the Jewish merchants as rivals and claimed the Jews were disrupting business in rural areas. As a result, the May Laws stated the Jewish population was restricted from settling outside of towns. Real estate sold to Jews outside of towns was revoked, and the Jews were forbidden from trading on certain days. Police were tasked with ensuring the May Laws were followed, which led to the continued harassment of Jews. The laws were finally taken away in 1917.

Franco-Russian Alliance of 1891–1894

In 1875, France faced the prospect of war against Germany. Eventually, Russia and Britain were able to force Germany to back down from starting a war. While France and Germany were experiencing tensions, France engendered friendly relations with Russia. By the end of the 1880s, Russia had received a few large loans from France. In 1892, the Russians and French signed a military convention that stipulated the two countries would support each other in the event of a German attack. By that point, Germany had grown to become a formidable power that was looking to preserve and increase its territory. In 1882, Germany formed the Triple Alliance with Austria-Hungary and Italy.

As the years passed, Russo-German relations began to deteriorate, which only pushed Russia and France closer. In 1894, the Russo-France military alliance was formalized.

The Franco-Russian alliance was mutually beneficial, as France was able to increase its colonial powers with Russia's help, while France helped Russia expand into Manchuria. While Russia was the dominant power in the alliance at first, the tsarist government took out a number of large loans from France, which meant Russia became financially dependent on France.

This alliance would prove to have serious consequences during the First World War, and Russia's financial dependence would cause the alliance to become unpopular in the future.

The Construction of the Trans-Siberian Railway

For years, Russia's railway was left in a deplorable state and eventually became ineffective, which was plainly demonstrated during the devastating famine in 1891. However, Alexander III found a way to fix that. He personally appointed ministers to supervise the construction of a massive railway system. Today, the railway connects western Russia to eastern Russia. It is still the longest railway line in the world, stretching about 5,772 miles long. It starts in Moscow and ends in the city of Vladivostok, which is located by the Sea of Japan.

The building began in 1891 and was finally completed in 1916. While the railway was still being built, adventurers came to see the progress. They eagerly wrote about the sights and adventures they encountered, which only increased the excitement surrounding the project.

Construction of the Trans-Siberian Railway.
https://commons.wikimedia.org/wiki/File:Construction_of_the_Transsiberian_Railway.jpg

The railway made it easier to transport grain from Siberia to Moscow and was used by the military during the Russo-Japanese War. It also allowed peasants to migrate from Russia and Ukraine to Siberia. However, the railway was heavily criticized, as it was alleged that greedy bureaucrats exaggerated the costs of construction to make more money. The project was allegedly poorly planned and not properly supervised. It was also a somewhat fragile system, as it couldn't handle heavy traffic when it was needed during the Russo-Japanese War.

Alexander III's Death and Legacy

Alexander III died in 1894 of nephritis, a terminal kidney illness. He was succeeded by his son, Nicholas II. He left behind a contradictory legacy, as many today remember him as a harsh autocrat who strengthened his rule at the people's expense. Much of his work was left unfinished, and his son was unprepared to take on such an important role in Russian politics.

While there are many who would paint Alexander III in an unflattering light, he managed to keep peaceful relationships with most of his neighbors and stabilize the economy. He was also known as a loving husband and devoted father. Unfortunately, his unwillingness to keep up with the times may have been his greatest weakness. Many claim his son had not been properly equipped with the skills and training he needed to rule Russia.

Alexander III clung to the old way of doing things, especially the autocratic monarchy, at a time when the world was being influenced by modern and radical thoughts. Russia's autocracy bloomed, while the vast majority of its people were uneducated and needed the protection of a strong monarchy. The world was changing quickly, and the Russian monarchy wasn't willing to make compromises or evolve, which eventually led to its violent downfall.

PART THREE: WWI and the Russian Revolution (1914–1922)

Chapter 7: Tsar Nicholas II and the February Revolution

For decades, the Romanovs ruled under an autocracy. Some of the Russian monarchs were exceptional leaders who brought the Enlightenment to Russia, making it a great country that rivaled some of the most advanced nations in Europe. However, their total autocracy was sometimes brutally enforced, which earned the suspicion and sometimes hatred of their subjects.

Radical new ideas swept Europe, bringing the Russian ruling dynasty's failures to the forefront. Eventually, those revolutionary ideas would become a reality and lead to the downfall of the Russian royal family. In a stunning sequence of events, Russia and the world would be left reeling as a new government took over and Russia's most prominent family faced a firing squad.

Nicholas II

Nicholas II was the oldest son of Alexander III and was born in 1868. One of Alexander III's greatest failures was not adequately preparing his heir for the throne. When Nicholas II took the throne in 1894, he didn't have enough government experience to take on the task set before him. Alexander III believed he would live a long life and was reluctant to make his son take on too many responsibilities within the government. It was suggested that Nicholas II should at least join the Siberian Railway Committee, but Alexander III refused, as he believed his son wasn't ready for such tasks.

A few months before his coronation, Nicholas became engaged to Princess Alix of Hesse-Darmstadt, who converted to Russian Orthodoxy and took the name Alexandra Feodorovna. Nicholas and Alexandra married shortly after Alexander III died, and Alexandra gave Nicholas the confidence he needed to rule. They were a happy couple and had four children: Grand Duchesses Olga, Tatiana, Maria, Anastasia, and Tsarevich Alexei, who was afflicted with hemophilia.

Nicholas II.

Nicholas reportedly deeply distrusted his closest advisors but was incapable of ruling without them. While he largely lacked the skills needed to rule Russia, he maintained many of his father's policies and busied himself with the government's administration. While he was fascinated by the notion of a constitutional monarchy like the one practiced in Britain, he did not seek to change the Russian government that much.

Shortly after he inherited the throne, a delegation of peasants approached him with proposals for reforms, including the suggestion that he institute a constitutional monarchy. The reforms would have made life better for his subjects, especially the peasants, but Nicholas angrily rejected their suggestions and claimed he would uphold his absolute power. This was an attitude he shared with many of his predecessors, but it would lead to his downfall.

Nicholas II was coronated on May 26th, 1896, and the next day, a large festival was held in Khodynka in Moscow, as it was large enough to host most of Moscow's citizens. The festival boasted food, free beer, and souvenirs. However, rumors quickly spread there would not be enough food for everyone, which led to a stampede. This led to the death of over one thousand people and came to be known as the Khodynka tragedy. The tragedy was seen as a bad omen, especially since it happened after Nicholas II's coronation, and he found it difficult to gain popularity with his subjects.

The French ambassador's gala had been planned for that night, but Nicholas II wanted to refrain from attending so he could pray for those who died at the festival. He was eventually persuaded to attend since his family believed he risked insulting the French if he didn't attend. As a result, he was viewed as a callous and uncaring monarch, which only exacerbated his unpopularity.

Russo-Japanese War (1904–1905)

At the beginning of the 20th century, Russia was an influential world power with massive territories in Europe and Asia, while Japan was a powerful force in Asia. During this time, there was a drive for European countries to gain more colonial territories. Nicholas II was affected by this attitude and didn't want Russia to be left out. He wanted to expand Russia's borders to include the Liaodong and Korean peninsulas, as these regions would provide Russia with a much-needed warm-water port. The Japanese wanted to limit Russian influence in those areas and instead offered Russia control of Manchuria (located in China). The deal would allow Japan to keep its influence over Korea. Russia refused, and the Japanese decided to go to war. The Russo-Japanese War attracted international attention and set the stage for World War I.

The war was incredibly brutal, and the Russians were accused of looting and burning several villages, as well as raping and killing hundreds of women. Over 150,000 people died on both sides, and 20,000 Chinese civilians also lost their lives. Eventually, the war came to an end in 1905 with the Treaty of Portsmouth, which was overseen by US President Theodore Roosevelt, who later won a Nobel Peace Prize for his efforts. The Russian army sustained many embarrassing losses during the war, and the public blamed Nicholas II for the army's shortcomings. The war ended in a crushing defeat for the Russians and led to serious consequences for the Russian monarchy.

Revolution of 1905

During 1905, social and political unrest spread throughout the Russian Empire. As opposition mounted, the autocracy faced increasing challenges that it could not overcome without giving in to some of the protestors' demands. After a year of near-constant mutinies, unrest, and strikes, Nicholas II was forced to institute a number of reforms to hold onto his power. Unfortunately, the Revolution of 1905 would not be the end of the calls for reform.

Several problems within Russian society caused the revolution. While peasants had finally been emancipated, their freedoms were still severely restricted. They earned very little money and weren't allowed to sell their land. Russian nationalism forced many minorities into lesser positions within the empire, and they weren't allowed to vote or join the army. They also had limited access to schools. Meanwhile, the working class blamed the government for failing to protect them since they weren't allowed to form unions or go on strike. Discipline became less restrictive at Russian universities, with students becoming exposed to radical new ideas from Europe. While these problems had plagued Russia periodically throughout history, they all finally coalesced to form a much larger problem that became fuel for a sustained revolution.

Bloody Sunday

Nicholas II's autocratic government quickly lost popularity and support due to the unpopular war with Japan and increasing corruption within the government. Although political and social parties petitioned for change, they were continuously rejected, which led them to adopt different tactics.

On January 22nd, 1905, an Orthodox priest named Georgy Gapon led a workers' march with the aim of delivering their petitions directly to the tsar. The workers were allegedly warned not to advance past a certain point that was guarded by troops. When the people didn't listen, the troops opened fire, which led to the deaths of many of the protestors. The march turned into a massacre that would come to be known as Bloody Sunday.

The massacre would be the start of a series of strikes, riots, and uprisings that formed the Revolution of 1905. The government claimed that about 96 died and 333 were injured, but those numbers were likely skewed. Some numbers go as high as fifteen thousand deaths. Whatever loyalty the public still held toward the autocratic government quickly died out during the revolution.

The Duma

To bring an end to the revolution, Nicholas II agreed to institute an elected national legislative assembly: the Duma. The Duma was an elected representative body consisting of a number of peasants, workers, and professionals who were supposed to help make decisions on behalf of all of Russia.

Despite his promises, Nicholas II wasn't happy about the Duma and wanted to make sure he would be able to hold onto all of his power. As a result, the Duma was made up of two chambers: one that would be made up of elected officials, while the other would be made up of officials chosen by the tsar. Nicholas II retained his absolute autocracy and gave his part of the Duma the right to veto any decisions made by the elected part. Initially, many hoped the Duma would allow Russia to become a democracy, but Nicholas II crippled the institution before it even began. The people recognized it was an empty gesture. The Duma went through multiple changes, and by 1917, there had been four different versions of the institution.

The first Duma mostly consisted of officials who were angry with the tsar. However, it became clear they wouldn't be consulted on any important matters, and the first Duma was shut down after only two months.

The second Duma lasted for a few months in 1907 but was dissolved when they opposed a series of reforms proposed by one of Nicholas II's ministers. The third Duma consisted of officials who were kinder to the tsar, but the fourth Duma, which was created in 1912, was critical of the tsar and his government. The fourth Duma forced the tsar to abdicate in 1917 and was turned into the Russian Provisional Government.

Russia and WWI

World War I changed the world and weakened several empires. The Russian Empire would not survive the conflict. It wasn't conquered by an enemy power; rather, it crumbled from within. In 1914, Tsar Nicholas II confidently declared war on Austria-Hungary and Germany. At that time, the Russian Empire ruled over a large portion of territory that stretched from Central Europe to the Pacific to the edge of the Arctic and Afghanistan. However, Russia was far behind the rest of Europe when it came to industrialism. Russia's factories and industry weren't fast enough to properly sustain the massive Imperial Russian Army. The Russians entered the war with outdated weapons and limited bullets. Many soldiers had to go into battle without weapons and were forced to pick up guns dropped by dead soldiers.

Nicholas II was also determined to lead his troops in battle, but he didn't have the skills or experience to do so successfully. To make matters worse, Nicholas II entrusted Russia to his wife, Alexandra, who was extremely unpopular with the Russians and increasingly influenced by the controversial mad monk Grigori Rasputin.

As the war dragged on, Russia experienced a series of terrible defeats. Over one million Russian soldiers were killed in the first year alone. The officer corps was severely impacted, which ultimately weakened the entire army. In 1915, the Russian troops were forced to retreat, leading to an influx of refugees fleeing to Russian cities. Inflation soared, food stocks were emptied, and the Russian government was burdened by an increasingly desperate population.

On March 3rd, 1918, Russia signed a treaty with the Central Powers that finally ended Russia's participation in the war. By then, a new government had taken over the country, and the Russian economy was in shambles.

Grigori Rasputin

When Princess Alix visited Russia before her engagement to Nicholas, she made several bad impressions on the Russians, especially on Alexander III and his wife. They initially opposed the match, but once Alexander III's health began to fail, they reluctantly changed their minds.

When Alexandra (Princess Alix) became queen, she didn't improve her standing in the eyes of the Russian population. The people thought she was too German due to her brusque personality. Nonetheless, Nicholas II loved her deeply. When he left for war, he left her in charge. She quickly began making changes in the government, such as firing elected officials, which only turned more people against her.

Grigori Rasputin.
https://commons.wikimedia.org/wiki/File:Rasputin_PA.jpg

To make matters worse, she kept close company with the controversial priest Grigori Rasputin. In 1905, the royal couple approached the priest, who had a reputation as a holy man with prophetic and healing powers. They urged him to help their son, Tsarevich Alexei, who had hemophilia. Rasputin was repeatedly able to heal the young boy, which increased the royal family's dependency on him. Some contend that he used mystical powers or herbs and drugs to do so, although the more likely scenario is that the doctors' attention stressed Alexei out. Rasputin ordered the doctors away so he could "heal" the boy, which stopped them from giving Alexei aspirin, a blood thinner.

Alexandra heavily depended on Rasputin, and he gained a considerable amount of political and personal influence over her. Rasputin often had public fights with members of the clergy and loudly bragged about his ability to control the tsar and tsarina. Many prominent Russians demanded that he be removed from the court.

As Russia weakened during the war and the population suffered, many people blamed Alexandra and Rasputin. Vicious rumors spread about their relationship, with many claiming they were having an affair, which only served to weaken Nicholas II's already fragile image. Russian nobles murdered Rasputin on December 30th, 1916. By then, the Russian public had lost all respect for the Romanov government.

The February Revolution

During the war, food distribution and transport became more inefficient, which led to food shortages, despite the fact there was more than enough food to feed the population. The Duma was unable to influence the tsar to change, and factory workers began to strike since they needed higher wages to keep up with the rising price of food. On International Women's Day (which began on March 8th, 1917, but was actually February 23rd, 1917, on the Julian calendar), tens of thousands of workers, mothers, and children marched in the streets of Petrograd to demand food. Soldiers were ordered to suppress the march using any means necessary. Many people died, and soldiers eventually stopped fighting and joined the protestors instead.

February Revolution in Petrograd.
https://commons.wikimedia.org/wiki/File:International_Women%27s_Day_-_February_Revolution_-_Petrograd.jpg

Throughout the war, Nicholas II refused to address the problems in his empire and either didn't understand or realize how bad things were going. Finally, the army revolted, and Nicholas II's generals persuaded him to step away from the throne. Nicholas left the throne to his younger brother, Michael, who chose not to take it. This brought a decisive end to the Romanov dynasty.

Aftermath

On March 12th, just days after the February Revolution, the Duma turned into the Russian Provisional Government and called for Nicholas II's abdication. The Romanov government was all but dissolved, and the royal family was deposed and imprisoned. Meanwhile, the provisional government instituted new rights, such as equality before the law, freedom of speech, and the right to form unions and strike. It hoped to prevent a violent revolution. A young lawyer named Alexander Kerensky helped to establish the new program and acted as the minister of war.

During this time, Russia was still involved in World War I, which was extremely unpopular with the Russian public. The war weakened Russia's already failing economy and made food shortages more common. Even though the unpopular tsar and his family were no longer in power, Russia was still in a freefall, with unrest becoming increasingly widespread. Desperate peasants were moved to loot food storages and farms, and riots broke out in almost every major city. The people weren't happy, and the provisional government was struggling to solve the problems.

Meanwhile, Germany wanted to remove Russia from the war and recognized the provisional government was struggling. In order to destabilize Russia, it helped the leader of the Bolsheviks return from exile on a secret train. Almost as soon as he arrived, he began increasing Bolshevik influence, which would lead to more revolutions.

The Execution of the Romanovs

When Alexander III died, Nicholas II became tsar. He was shocked and unprepared. Reportedly, he asked one of his advisors, "What is going to happen to me ... to all of Russia?" A little over two decades later, he and his family were imprisoned by the Bolsheviks, a far-left Marxist group.

The Russian imperial family in 1916 (Alexei is absent from the picture).
https://commons.wikimedia.org/wiki/File:Russian_Imperial_family_in_1916.jpg

Following the October Revolution, Nicholas II finally recognized the danger he and his family were in. He petitioned France and Britain to take them, but both countries refused, despite the fact that Alexandra was Queen Victoria's granddaughter. This meant they were at the mercy of the Bolshevik government. The family was imprisoned and moved to several different houses. They were harassed by soldiers and forced to live in relative squalor. Despite their docile acceptance of their circumstances, they were still a problem to the Bolsheviks, who feared the royal family would somehow escape and cause problems. Nicholas II and Alexandra both maintained they would be saved. And they were right in a way, as the White Army, which fought against the Bolsheviks, sought to rescue them. They didn't make it in time.

With the White Army approaching, the Bolsheviks knew something had to be done. On July 17th, 1918, the family was told they were going to be moved again. Little did they know that they and their servants were going to be marched to the basement to be executed.

The Romanovs had cleverly sewn jewels, religious icons, and money into their clothes to use in case the family ever escaped. But what should have been a quick execution took twenty minutes.

After the initial onslaught, all of the children were still alive due to the number of jewels and other items sewn into their garments. Tatiana, Maria, and Anastasia were wearing pounds of jewels. The executioners shot, stabbed, and beat the family until they were dead. (Although imposters sprang up later on, the Romanov family and their servants all died in the attack.)

The bodies were taken to a mineshaft and drenched in sulfuric acid. However, the mine shaft was not as deep as the ringleader had envisioned. The bodies were moved about until it was finally decided it would be best to bury them. One of the graves was found in 1979, although an investigation didn't take place until 1991. The other grave, which held Alexei and Maria, was found in 2007.

The world was shocked by the murder of the royal family. This act of violence defined the Russian Revolution, not the political victories that Vladimir Lenin and the Bolsheviks had worked so hard to attain.

Chapter 8: The October Revolution and the Russian Civil War

Vladimir Lenin and the Bolsheviks viewed the monarchy as a cancer that impeded Russia's growth and the welfare of Russian workers. They fought hard to bring an end to the autocratic monarchy, but once they did, they found that Russia would be harder to reform than they had imagined. The economy was in a mess, as Russia had fought in the seemingly endless Great War, and the provisional government wasn't willing to give up its power without a fight.

The Bolsheviks quickly gained power and popularity with the people and were able to stage their own revolution, which turned their government into a reality. When Russia finally left World War I, many suspected Russia was on the road to recovery. However, more climactic events would rip through the country until it was plunged into a terrible civil war.

Karl Marx and Communism

Karl Marx was born in 1818 in Prussia. He later attended the University of Bonn, where he was arrested for dueling with another student and drunkenness. He then enrolled at the University of Berlin, where he studied philosophy and law. Marx was deeply influenced by the philosophy of professor G. W. F Hegel. While he was in university, he became involved with the Young Hegelians, which was a movement that opposed many European political establishments. Marx was exposed to many radical ideas that later affected his work as a journalist.

Karl Marx.
https://commons.wikimedia.org/wiki/File:Karl_Marx.png

As a result, he was expelled by several European governments. In 1848, he worked with Friedrich Engels and completed *The Communist Manifesto*. The book introduced many new radical political concepts and claimed that socialism was the result of capitalism's failings. Their theories caused unrest and increased workers' movements, in which Marx participated. Marx's work swept throughout Europe and inspired countless political parties, including the Bolsheviks in Russia.

As the years passed, Marx developed his economic theories and worked as a journalist and revolutionary. In 1864, he helped to create the International Workingmen's Association and later published the first part of *Capital: A Critique of Political Economy*, which was a volume regarding his economic theory. He claimed that capitalism would always self-destruct and lead to communism. While Marx worked hard to finish the book, he never completed his work, as he died in 1883. He had no idea that his work would have such far-reaching consequences and eventually become the basis for Russia's socialist government.

The Rise of the Bolsheviks

The Bolsheviks were a far-left, revolutionary Marxist faction. It was founded by Vladimir Lenin, who split from the Mensheviks, one of the most influential parties of the Russian Socialist Movement. Lenin promoted the split when he wrote a political pamphlet entitled "What Is to Be Done?" The pamphlet was outlawed in Russia, which had strict censorship laws.

Lenin strongly believed a revolution would only occur if it was led by professional leaders who were extremely dedicated to Karl Marx's principles. In 1903, the Russian Social Democratic Labor Party (RSDLP) met at the Second Party Congress. During this time, Lenin and Julius Martov, another prominent member of the party, had a disagreement about the party's membership rules. Lenin aimed to create a group of professional revolutionaries who devoted their full strength to overthrow the tsarist government. The disagreements grew and led to a decisive split within the party.

The Bolsheviks played a small part in the Revolution of 1905 and went on to strengthen their ranks over the years. They eventually created their own official party in 1912, signifying their complete separation from other socialist parties. There were several disagreements within the party as to how Russia should be governed once the party took power, but their political goal remained the same. They wanted to overthrow the tsarist government and bring about complete social change. Many viewed the unequal treatment of the workers as immoral and claimed that social classes had to end. Lenin's works promoted the goal of a group of highly trained revolutionaries overthrowing the government and eventually giving power to a socialist party that would govern more effectively.

When World War I broke out and the tsarist regime floundered, the revolution the Bolsheviks had been waiting for became a reality.

Vladimir Lenin

Vladimir Lenin was born in 1870 to a middle-class family. At the time, his name was Vladimir Ilyich Ulyanov. He was one of six siblings and attended high school, which was impressive for the time. In 1887, Lenin's older brother was executed when it was revealed he had been part of a plot to assassinate Alexander III. This exposed Lenin to radical political ideas that would eventually define his life.

During his childhood, the government clamped down on education. Since Lenin's father was an inspector of schools, the family was targeted by the government, and Lenin's father was threatened with early retirement. This likely contributed to Lenin's aversion to the tsarist regime.

While attending university, Lenin studied law but took part in a student protest that got him expelled. During this period, he began reading more radical literature, including the works of Karl Marx. When he finished university, he gained a law degree. By that time, he had already become a Marxist.

Vladimir Lenin giving a speech.
https://commons.wikimedia.org/wiki/File:Vladimir_Lenin_giving_a_speech.jpg

In the mid-1890s, Vladimir was arrested and exiled to Siberia. A few years later, after his exile ended, he moved to Germany and then Switzerland, where he was able to freely associate with other Marxists. Eventually, he adopted the name Lenin and became the founder of the Bolshevik Party.

Lenin claimed the First World War was a result of capitalism. The German government sent Lenin and several other Russian radicals back to Russia with the aim of destabilizing the government to bring an end to Russia's involvement in the war. Lenin immediately set his sights on overthrowing the Russian Provisional Government, which he claimed was a bourgeois dictatorship.

Leon Trotsky

Lev Davidovic Bronstein, or Leon Trotsky, was born in modern-day Ukraine in 1879. While still in school, he was introduced to Marxism, which would shape the rest of his life. In 1897, he became a founding member of the South Russian Workers' Union. Bronstein was eventually arrested for his political activities and exiled to Siberia. While in exile, he met and fell in love with a co-revolutionary named Alexandra Lvovna Tolstaya (the daughter of Leo Tolstoy). The couple had two children together. In 1902, Bronstein was able to escape from exile, even though it meant he had to leave his family behind. He used the name Leon Trotsky on his forged papers, and he continued to use the name for the rest of his life.

Trotsky went to London, where he met Vladimir Lenin and joined the Socialist Democratic Party. While in London, he met Natalia Ivanovna, whom he married. The couple had two sons.

Leon Trotsky.
https://commons.wikimedia.org/wiki/File:Leon_Trotsky_Sailor.jpg

During those days, the Socialist Democratic Party fought over membership and leadership. Lenin wanted a small group of trained revolutionaries to control a large group of supporters, while Julius Martov wanted a more democratic organization. Trotsky remained neutral and tried to negotiate between the two sides, but many members chose to side with Lenin.

In 1905, Trotsky returned to Russia, where he became heavily involved in the Revolution of 1905. He was once again arrested and exiled. His actions endeared him to the party, and he managed to escape prison once again. Trotsky spent the next ten years in exile in Europe, where he wrote for Russian revolutionary journals.

When the tsarist government was overthrown, he went back to Russia to help solve some of the problems that arose after the revolution. However, he loudly criticized the Russian Provisional Government, which led to his arrest. This led Trotsky to join the Bolshevik Party.

During that time, Petrograd Soviet was the seat of the opposition to the Russian Provisional Government. After Trotsky joined the Bolsheviks, he was made the chairman of the Petrograd Soviet. He would go on to help Lenin and the Bolsheviks overthrow the provisional government. Trotsky also served in the Russian Civil War and became one of Stalin's biggest enemies.

Joseph Stalin

Ioseb Besarionis dze Jughashvili, better known as Joseph Stalin, was born in 1878 in Georgia. He later took on the name Stalin, which means "man of steel." Stalin was the only child of a shoemaker and a laundress. His father was an abusive alcoholic who regularly beat his son. While he was still a child, Stalin contracted smallpox, which left scars on his face for the rest of his life. While attending school, he became a Marxist and was eventually expelled in 1899.

Stalin actively took part in strikes and labor movements, which led him to join the Bolsheviks. During the early years of the party, he took part in bank robberies to raise money for the party. He was arrested multiple times and exiled to Siberia, as were many of his peers.

In 1906, he married Ekaterina Svanidze and fathered a son, Yakov, with whom Stalin was never particularly close. Ekaterina died soon after her son was born. In 1918, Stalin married Nadezhda "Nadya" Alliluyeva, the daughter of a revolutionary. They had two children, a daughter and a son. His daughter, Svetlana Alliluyeva, eventually defected to the United States in 1967. He fathered several illegitimate children, and Nadya eventually committed suicide while she was in her thirties.

Young Joseph Stalin.

While Lenin was in Switzerland, he arranged for Stalin to serve on the first Central Committee of the Bolshevik Party. Stalin was highly ambitious, and during the party's early days, he made sure to side with Lenin during party disputes. When the Bolsheviks became more prominent after the February Revolution, Stalin played a big part in helping them gain power. He eventually became one of the most prominent members of the party.

The Russian Provisional Government

By the time Lenin returned to Russia, the country as a whole was tired of the ravages of war. Lenin promoted the Bolshevik Party under the slogan, "Peace, Land, Bread," which greatly appealed to the war-weary Russians. Meanwhile, the provisional government was struggling to effectively combat all the problems Russia was facing, but several prominent Russians tried to make the provisional government work. However, after the monarchy was removed, there was a power vacuum, and many scrambled to enrich themselves. And despite the fact that most Russians were sick of the war, the provisional government kept Russia fighting on the front lines.

Eventually, Alexander Kerensky was left as the last head of the provisional government. He launched an offensive against the Austrians and Germans in 1917. It was a massive failure and caused an uproar in Russia. More and more soldiers began defecting from the army, and the Bolsheviks spread propaganda within the army, which turned sentiments against the provisional government. Kerensky responded by attempting to send all Bolshevik soldiers to the worst battlefronts, which forced the soldiers to rise against the Russian Provisional Government. These rebellions were known as the July Days. Soldiers and sailors gathered in front of the Tauride Palace in an attempt to overthrow the provisional government. While the rebellion was eventually suppressed, the Russian Provisional Government was on its last legs and wouldn't survive for much longer. It would eventually be overthrown during the October Revolution.

The October Revolution

On October 24th and 25th, 1917 (according to the Julian calendar), Lenin finally made his move against the Russian Provisional Government. He initiated a coup and called for a Soviet government instead. His goal was to replace the bourgeois government with a government controlled by councils consisting of peasants, workers, and soldiers. His party had been gaining popularity after the February Revolution, especially since many Russians wanted to leave the First World War. The coup was almost bloodless, and the Bolsheviks took control of key locations in Petrograd and established a new government.

Workers and soldiers had long been demanding complete change, which provided a good basis for Lenin's long-awaited revolution. He had already set up a volunteer paramilitary force called the Red Guards, which helped him during the coup. He also spent months arranging for workers, soldiers, sailors, and peasants to become effective Red Guards. As soon as the Bolsheviks attained power, they announced Soviet rule with Lenin as their ruler. This was a remarkable feat, and Lenin became the first communist state leader in history.

Bolshevik Government

After the coup, the Bolsheviks set up the Council of People's Commissars, with Lenin as the chairman. Trotsky became the commissar for foreign affairs. The Bolshevik government's first order of business was to bring an end to Russia's involvement in World War I. Trotsky was placed in charge of making peace with the Germans and finding a way out of the war. The Germans, who had a hand in helping many prominent revolutionaries return to Russia, had been hoping for this outcome and were ready with a list of reparations and territory demands.

However, Trotsky didn't want to give in to German demands and advised Lenin to reject them. He suggested they wait for a while to see if the Allies defeated Germany or if Germany was forced to withdraw from the war due to internal conflict. Lenin disagreed, as he wanted to bring a quick end to the war that was proving to be a continuous drain on Russian resources and morale. He wanted to focus on building the new Soviet government instead.

In March 1918, the Bolshevik government signed the Treaty of Brest-Litovsk with Austria-Hungary, Germany, Bulgaria, and the Ottoman Empire. The move cost them a million square miles worth of territory. Trotsky resigned from his post as commissar for foreign affairs.

The Bolsheviks had recently set up the Red Army, and Lenin appointed Trotsky as its leader. Trotsky shined in this role and was given the task of bringing an end to the anti-Bolshevik movement known as the White Movement.

Lenin immediately set about instituting many of the Marxist reforms he had always dreamed about and was on his way to establishing a strong communist government. He also established the Cheka, which was Russia's first secret police. The Cheka was used to silence any opposers within the Bolshevik Party and any political rivals. In response, a political rival shot Lenin in the shoulder and neck in 1918.

The Cheka was given permission to institute a campaign of mass executions. This time came to be known as the Red Terror. Within two months, the Cheka had executed about 100,000 "class enemies." Those who were executed included tsarist supporters, members of the former upper class, and Bolshevik opposers. The events after the October Revolution eventually led to the Russian Civil War.

The Anti-Bolshevik Movement

Ever since the Bolsheviks took power, they were opposed by a number of different factions. However, it wasn't until the Treaty of Brest-Litovsk that anti-Bolshevik factions were moved to take action. The White Army was formed from members of non-Bolshevik socialists, liberals, army generals, former landowners, pro-monarchists, and others who shared a hatred of the Bolsheviks. The White Army controlled large parts of the former Russian Empire and strengthened the army through conscriptions and foreign support.

Many Western Allies were disgusted by the actions of the Bolshevik government and supported the White Army. These Western countries were concerned the Bolsheviks would ally with Germany. The Bolsheviks had also promised to default on massive foreign loans, and the Western Allies were increasingly afraid the revolutionary ideas that had taken hold in Russia would spread. Winston Churchill famously claimed that Bolshevism had to be strangled in its cradle.

To that end, Western Allied countries sent the White Army troops and supplies. The Allies had also given Russia a huge amount of war supplies and were worried those supplies would be given to the Germans, which would prolong the war. As a result, foreign troops were sent to Russia, where they frequently clashed with the Red Army.

The Russian Civil War

The Russian Civil War broke out in 1917, with Trotsky leading the Red Army on behalf of the Bolsheviks. In 1918, the Romanovs were executed, which brought an end to the efforts to restore Nicholas II to the throne. Trotsky proved to be a capable leader who led his army to victory. This was no easy feat, as several Bolshevik officials, including Lenin, often overturned Trotsky's strategies and efforts. He also had to fight the war on sixteen different fronts, as the White Army came at him from all sides. The war was brutal, and about 300,000 people died. The Cheka continued the Red Terror during this time; according to estimations, it may have killed over a million people.

During the war, Lenin instituted a number of policies that came to be known as war communism. These temporary policies allowed Lenin to strengthen his position and defeat his enemies. Lenin nationalized all manufacturing and industries and took grain from the peasants to feed the Red Army. As a result, industries and manufacturing plummeted, and the grain shortage eventually caused famine. This led to mass poverty and unrest. Many peasants and workers were affected, which caused some to long for the days of the monarchy, but those views couldn't be expressed freely due to the Cheka's reign of terror.

The Red Army managed to win the war in 1920, and the White Army was forced to surrender. Bolshevik rule and the Soviet government were firmly entrenched.

The Russian economy had been ravaged by the war, as infrastructure had been destroyed. A large amount of the skilled and educated population fled Russia, and a disastrous drought caused disease and famine. By that time, the Russian government was near complete ruin.

After the Russian Civil War, a treaty was signed between Ukraine, Belarus, the Transcaucasus, and Russia in 1922. This led to Lenin forming the Union of Soviet Republics (USSR). Lenin was the first head of the USSR, but he wouldn't hold onto the position for long, as he suffered from a series of strokes between 1922 and 1924. During this time, Stalin began gaining power, and it wouldn't be long until the USSR ushered in a new era in Russian history.

PART FOUR: The Journey from Communist Russia to the Russian Republic (1922–2022)

Chapter 9: The Union of Soviet Socialist Republics (USSR)

For years, revolutionaries like Vladimir Lenin worked to bring an end to the tsarist government. When they finally achieved this goal, they were able to build a government based on their Marxist ideals. However, they were forced to contend with serious opposition that threatened their regime. As the first communist state in history, they were left to navigate unprecedented challenges that tested their intelligence and ingenuity.

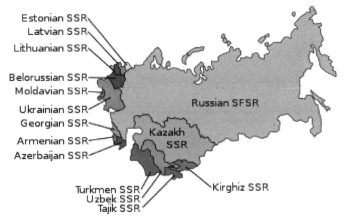

Map of the USSR.

Special:Contributions/Saul ip. Derivative work by Σ, CC BY-SA 3.0
<https://creativecommons.org/licenses/by-sa/3.0>, via Wikimedia Commons;
https://commons.wikimedia.org/wiki/File:Map_of_USSR_with_SSR_names.svg

After the Russian Civil War, the Bolsheviks' opposition was defeated, but the state was on the brink of collapse. To make matters worse, Lenin's health was failing, and the USSR was rocked by the rise of an ambitious official named Joseph Stalin, who was determined to rise to the top no matter what it took.

Formation of the USSR

On December 29th, 1922, delegates from Russia, Ukraine, Belarus, and the Transcaucasus met and signed the Declaration of the Creation of the USSR. In 1924, Britain formally recognized the USSR, and a Soviet Constitution was approved that legitimized the 1922 meeting. The Bolsheviks could finally get on with creating their new government, and many hoped the brutalities of the past years would be forgotten.

The Bolsheviks, led by Vladimir Lenin, concentrated on restructuring every part of Russia. This included reforming the economy and aimed to provide basic services like electricity to the country. A plan was developed for the construction of twenty regional power stations, hydroelectric power plants, and electric-powered enterprises. This plan would eventually provide the basis for the later five-year plans, which we will touch on in more depth later. Any type of capitalist venture or production was viciously suppressed, as the Bolsheviks wanted to achieve total communism. The policies that had been enacted during the Russian Civil War had led to unrest and desperate poverty. This caused the government to rethink its strategy, and Lenin was forced to come up with the New Economic Policy.

There was little time to enjoy the political victory of the USSR's establishment since there was mounting opposition from within the country as poverty and unrest rose. To make matters worse, tensions rose within the Bolshevik Party, as ministers disagreed about how the new government should be administered and controlled.

Kronstadt Rebellion

Russia had been in a near-constant crisis ever since the outbreak of the First World War. The people had been forced to participate in a terrible war, sending their male relatives off to become soldiers in an army that couldn't even provide them with guns. After that, Russia went through numerous revolutions, rebellions, and uprisings. When the Bolsheviks rose to power, many people hoped that things would improve.

While the Bolsheviks removed Russia from the war, a brand-new war started a few months later that hit a lot closer to home. Once again, the Russian people were subjected to new changes that only worsened their situation since they were forced to adhere to the policies of war communism. Much of the population had been unaware of communism, Karl Marx, and socialist parties before the Bolsheviks took power.

Grain seizures and bans on free trade caused serious distress throughout Russia, as peasants and townspeople suffered greatly. Production fell to shockingly low levels. This caused widespread dissent and strikes, which only made the problem worse. The Bolsheviks struggled to keep the unrest contained, but they were hit by yet another stunning blow before they could achieve their aims. In 1921, the soldiers and sailors stationed at Kronstadt started a massive uprising.

Kronstadt was an island fortress that guarded the key city of Petrograd. The uprising was surprising because the soldiers of Kronstadt had been some of the most loyal Bolshevik supporters during the revolution. Trotsky himself had dubbed them the heroes of the revolution. However, the soldiers and sailors there were moved to action due to the conditions the people faced. When they heard and saw what the country was going through, they fought against the regime they had helped gain power.

The soldiers formed a Provisional Revolutionary Committee and sent the government a list of economic, political, and social demands. The rebels also asserted they wanted soviets without Bolsheviks and established an anti-Bolshevik newspaper. They claimed the Bolsheviks were worse than the tsarist government. However, the rebels also made some good points and urged the Bolsheviks to ease the policies of war communism to bring relief to the people.

The Bolsheviks responded harshly and sent a powerful force to crush the rebellion. Many supporters of the Bolshevik Party were disgusted by the handling of the rebellion, and Lenin quickly realized that things needed to change.

The New Economic Policy

During the Russian Civil War, Lenin introduced a series of temporary policies that came to be known as war communism. Some of these policies requisitioned surplus grain from peasants to feed the Red Army, which caused serious food shortages and famine. The problem was exacerbated by a severe drought that plagued Russia in 1920 and 1921. When the crops failed, there was no surplus grain left to solve the shortage, and thousands suffered. Lenin recognized the need to ease some of his communist policies and introduced the New Economic Policy (NEP) in 1921.

The NEP was a massive departure from many of the ideals that were upheld in the Bolshevik Party, and many officials opposed this move. Essentially, the NEP allowed elements of free trade and capitalism. The policy of grain requisitioning was brought to an end, which brought relief to the peasants. Russian farmers were permitted to buy and sell their goods, leading to the development of a merchant class called "Nepmen."

While many Russians were thrilled by the changes, the NEP caused turmoil within the Bolshevik Party. The Bolshevik government still held control of the most important elements of the economy, such as industries, finance, and banking. Still, many Bolsheviks felt the NEP was a betrayal of their socialist beliefs.

Since farmers were allowed to sell their surplus goods again, they were motivated to produce more, which led to a rise in agricultural production. While the NEP didn't singlehandedly save the Russian economy, it brought much-needed relief to the people and is generally regarded as a success.

Aftermath of Lenin's Death

Between the years of 1922 and 1924, Lenin was afflicted by a series of strokes that severely impacted his health. He struggled to speak and used all his strength to govern. As his life neared its end, he feared what would happen to the government he had helped to create. He was keenly aware of the dangerous forces within his own party. During the last few months of his life, he wrote a few essays about the Communist Party's corruption. He recognized that Stalin was a dangerous individual and suggested that he be removed from his high-ranking office. The essays came to be known as "Lenin's Testament."

Lenin died in January 1924. His body was moved several times before it was embalmed and displayed in Lenin's Tomb in Red Square, Moscow. Close to a million people lined up in the blistering cold to pay their respects to their former leader. St. Petersburg, which had been renamed Petrograd, was then called Leningrad in Lenin's honor. Despite all the honors that were heaped on his name, his advice about Stalin went largely unheeded.

Lenin's Mausoleum.
Jorge Láscar from Melbourne, Australia, CC BY 2.0
<https://creativecommons.org/licenses/by/2.0>, via Wikimedia Commons;
https://commons.wikimedia.org/wiki/File:Lenin%27s_Mausoleum_(19775699420).jpg

When Lenin suffered his first stroke, there were questions about who would be his successor. Many assumed that Trotsky would take his place since he had a strong record of service, but he had also offended many important officials. Stalin was one of those Trotsky had offended, and he supported the opposition against Trotsky. Stalin had been appointed as the general secretary of the Central Committee, which allowed him to control party member appointments. He used his position to place his allies in strategic positions.

Lenin had supported Trotsky over Stalin, but his rapidly declining health prevented his efforts from being successful. When Lenin died, Stalin politically outmaneuvered Trotsky and took control of the Communist Party. Stalin became the dictator of the USSR, while Trotsky was slowly pushed out of the government.

What Lenin had warned had come to pass.

Joseph Stalin in Power

Stalin was a dictator who ruled through terror and used whatever means necessary to get rid of his opposition. The beginning of his reign seemed promising, as he introduced a series of five-year plans that were supposed to revitalize Russia's economy and turn it into a modern communist powerhouse. When his plans weren't well received, he resorted to exiling, executing, and punishing those who voiced dissent. He implemented policies of forced collectivization that led to widespread poverty and hunger. Stalin employed secret police and created a Gulag system, which was constituted of forced labor camps. Neighbors were encouraged to spy on each other and report any crimes or opposition to the new regime.

Stalin enforced his absolute power and used propaganda to present himself as the perfect leader. He built himself into Soviet culture by renaming cities in his honor, rewriting history books to embellish his achievements, and putting his name in the national anthem. He made sure he was flattered in art, literature, and music. Stalin's regime also controlled the media and exercised extreme censorship.

Leon Trotsky was the only person who seemed to be able to stop Stalin, and he never stopped trying to oppose Stalin's government. By 1928, Trotsky had been pushed out of the government, and his achievements were discredited. He was then banished from the Soviet Union. Although Trotsky couldn't return to his homeland, he continued writing about Stalin's abuses of power. Stalin retaliated by claiming that Trotsky was a traitor and an enemy of his people. Trotsky's allies were persecuted, and Trotsky was assassinated with an ice axe by a member of the secret police in 1940.

The Five-Year Plans

Stalin was an ambitious man who didn't let anything stand between him and the power he craved. When he finally became the leader of the USSR, he revealed his incredibly ambitious plans for the Soviet Union. He introduced a series of five-year plans that were aimed at developing the country's industry and collectivizing agriculture. The first plan began on October 1ˢᵗ, 1928. Stalin decided the entire economy needed to be reformed to keep pace with Western Europe. He believed that unless Russia caught up with its European neighbor, the country would be crushed by capitalist powers.

The first five-year plan focused on making agriculture more efficient by introducing mechanization and collectivization. New industrial centers were built in uninhabited areas that were rich in natural resources. More emphasis was placed on heavy industries as Russia prepared for a future industrialized war. This shift in focus led to a mass exodus from rural areas to cities, as people went in search of better lives and provided the workforce that the first five-year plan needed to succeed. However, the new labor force was completely unskilled and struggled to operate industrial machinery. Workers also had to endure terrible factory conditions that took a toll on human lives.

Furthermore, the collectivization of agriculture caused famine and unrest. The plan did lead to a significant increase in output, but it also failed terribly in key aspects. Millions had left behind their farms in search of a better life but found themselves trapped in factories and were forced to work in deplorable conditions. Those who had stayed behind were swept up in agricultural collectivization policies that eventually contributed to widespread famine.

Stalin's government placed the blame on kulaks (peasants who had benefited from the NEP and managed to amass a certain amount of wealth). The kulaks were viciously persecuted and were either killed or sent to the Gulag, where they were forced to work on Stalin's projects. Once the kulaks were out of the way, their land was given to the state to support collectivization.

Citizens in non-Russian parts of the Soviet Union also suffered. They were subject to Stalin's policies and soon felt the disastrous effects of the five-year plans. This led to a rift between Russians and non-Russians. To make matters worse, the policies led to a devastating famine in Ukraine called the Holodomor. The Soviet government failed to respond to the disaster, which led to Ukrainian resentment. Some argue whether this was genocide; sixteen countries believe it was. Up to five million died in Ukraine because of famine.

Despite the failures and suffering caused by the first five-year plan, Stalin continued with his second five-year plan. This allowed the Soviet Union to become one of the major steel-producing countries. There were several successes, such as the improvements made in communications and faster and more reliable railways. However, the second plan failed to live up to projected production levels.

The USSR would continue to use five-year plans until it was dissolved in 1991. Emphasis was put on production, and improvements were continually being made to improve production. For example, childcare was introduced so that mothers could focus on working harder in factories and in the fields. A system of incentives and punishments was also used to motivate people to work harder.

Moscow Trials

During his time as the leader of the USSR, Stalin conducted multiple political purges to rid himself of enemies. This led to numerous show trials, which were perfectly planned to result in Stalin's desired outcome. Political rivals, such as opponents to the Communist Party and Trotskyists, were tried at sham trials that served only to put on a show for the country. The Moscow trials occurred during the Great Purge, lasting from 1937 to 1938. These trials are perfect examples of Stalin's show trials.

The Moscow trials were a series of high-profile trials that put several influential communists on trial for treason. There were even prominent Americans who supported the trials and approved of the verdicts. It was a shocking spectacle designed to display Stalin's power and suppress any possible opposition to his government.

Stalin coerced several high-ranking communists, most of whom had served during the 1917 Revolution and Russian Civil War, into admitting they were traitors to the USSR. Some of these confessions were made after their loved ones were threatened. Most of the trials ended in executions and were transparently rigged. Despite their loyalty to the Russian communist cause, these officials had either supported Trotsky or refused to ally themselves with Stalin, which, in Stalin's eyes, were crimes worthy of death.

Once his rivals were gone, Stalin was able to rewrite history books and claimed many of their achievements as his own. This added to the mythification of his name and turned him into a living legend.

The Great Purge

Stalin worked for years to consolidate his power, and in 1929, he finally became the dictator of the USSR. However, his work was far from over. Many officials within the government began to challenge his authority while the danger of the Nazis in Germany and militarists in Japan were becoming a reality. Some historians claim Stalin initiated the Great Purge to unify the USSR and strengthen the country before those dangers could overpower Russia. However, others claim he wanted to maintain his position as dictator. Whatever his motives were, Stalin launched a violent campaign against his opposition, which included anyone who could possibly challenge his power. This meant members of Lenin's government and those who had supported Trotsky became targets.

Between 1936 and 1938, an estimated 750,000 people were executed. More than a million people were sent to the Gulag. The Moscow trials helped Stalin destroy his enemies' reputations and gave him a legitimate excuse to execute them. The Great Purge also came to be known as the Great Terror and left a lasting mark on the psyche of the Russian population.

The purge started in 1934 with the assassination of Sergei Kirov, a Bolshevik leader. Suddenly, the Bolsheviks found themselves at the mercy of the government they had helped to create.

While the purge started with the persecution of political officials, it soon stretched to include artists, peasants, ethnic minorities, foreigners, intellectuals, writers, and even soldiers. No one was safe. Thirty thousand soldiers of the Red Army were executed after Stalin became convinced they were planning to overthrow him. Stalin's brutality knew no bounds; he even created a law that stated families were liable for crimes committed by a family member. This meant that children from the age of twelve could be executed.

Those who were sent to the Gulag were subject to torture, horrific conditions, and execution, which means the number of people killed during the Great Purge likely exceeded 750,000.

The Great Purge was later condemned by Stalin's successor, but it was too late. Hundreds of thousands of people had died, and the people's spirits were broken. Entire groups of Russian society, such as writers and intellectuals, had been wiped out. It also ensured the people were dependent on the state and, by extension, Stalin.

Russian Society under the USSR

Russian society and culture went through numerous changes under the rule of the USSR. During the first few years after the revolution, artists enjoyed relative freedom, experimenting with various styles to create a unique style that would define Soviet art. Under Lenin, the government promoted art since they wanted it to be accessible to all people. However, the USSR kept a strict watch on intellectuals, including writers and artists. If artists criticized the USSR or seemed to be against the government, they faced exile, harsh punishments, execution, or work bans. The government supported many different trends, which led to an era of experimentation. Films were particularly encouraged since they could influence the illiterate public.

However, things became harder for artists under Stalin's rule. He encouraged the rise of socialist realism and suppressed other trends. Many writers were heavily persecuted during this time as well. It wouldn't be until the 1950s that censorship would be relaxed during the Khrushchev Thaw.

Chapter 10: The Great Patriotic War and the Cold War

When the USSR was formed, it became the first communist state in the world. Communists and socialists around the world had high hopes that it would succeed. However, the flaws in the system quickly became apparent, and the state fell short of the lofty ideals touted by the Bolsheviks. In reality, the road to pure communism was littered with famine, unrest, and violent political purges.

However, these events turned Russia into a major power. By the time the Second World War ended, both Russia and America emerged as prominent countries. They would eventually become locked in a conflict known as the Cold War.

Prelude to World War II

In 1938, France, the United Kingdom, and Italy signed the Munich Agreement with Germany, which gave Czechoslovakian territory to Germany. Since France had made a military pact with Czechoslovakia a few years prior, the Munich Agreement came to be known as the Munich Betrayal.

Germany, which was ruled by Adolf Hitler at the time, had been steadily growing in power and influence, despite the heavy war reparations it was forced to pay after the First World War. A year later, the Soviet Union signed a non-aggression pact with Nazi Germany. Later, it would be revealed at the Nuremberg trials that the Soviet Union and Nazi Germany planned to divide the territories of Poland, Lithuania, Romania, Finland, and Estonia between themselves.

On September 1st, 1939, Germany invaded Poland, which marked the beginning of the Second World War. Stalin launched his own invasion of Poland a few days later. Stalin also invaded and annexed parts of Romania, Estonia, Lithuania, and Latvia. There were some talks about the USSR joining the Axis Powers with Germany, Italy, and Japan. Stalin even went as far as to sign a neutrality pact with Japan, with whom Russia had been competing for interests in the Far East after the collapse of imperial China. However, Stalin wasn't satisfied with Germany's offers, and negotiations soon broke down. He sensed that some Germans were interested in invading the USSR, but he had no idea about Hitler's looming betrayal.

Operation Barbarossa

The non-aggression pact between Germany and the USSR was a blow to the Allied powers, as Russia and Germany had been enemies for years. The pact ensured that neither country would attack the other for at least ten years. Soon after Germany invaded Poland, Britain and France declared war on Germany. After a few months, Germany launched the Blitzkrieg, which means "lightning war." The Blitzkrieg was a surprise attack that consisted of rapid movements to put the enemy off-balance. With this tactic, Germany conquered the Netherlands, Luxembourg, France, and Belgium.

The USSR was busy negotiating an alliance with Germany, but Hitler likely never planned to honor the non-aggression pact with the USSR. He had his eye on expanding eastward and colonizing the USSR, especially Ukraine. This was all part of his Lebensraum ("living space") goal, which aimed to ensure the survival of the German people by allowing them to colonize racially inferior territories. The Nazis believed the Slavic people were inferior to the Aryan race, the false idea that the original speakers of proto-Indo-European languages were superior to everyone else.

Operation Barbarossa lines of attack.

In 1941, Hitler launched Operation Barbarossa, which was the German invasion of the USSR. The operation aimed to advance from the port of Archangel along the Volga River to the port of Astrakhan. Hitler had one of the most impressive invasion forces at his disposal. It consisted of about 80 percent of his Wehrmacht (the Nazis' armed forces). Hitler hoped to quickly subdue the USSR and was buoyed by the success of the Blitzkrieg.

The invasion was especially brutal, as armed SS death squads followed the army and killed civilians, especially Jews. German forces were also ordered to kill any Soviet officers. Many Soviet prisoners of war were executed, which went against international war protocols. The Soviet Army was caught largely unaware, which allowed the Germans to make large territorial gains.

Despite their surprise, the Soviet Army was able to make a strong defense. For some reason, Hitler decided to order his army to press on toward Moscow instead of Ukraine. The Wehrmacht managed to capture Kyiv and besiege Leningrad. Russia's situation looked desperate, especially since the citizens of Leningrad began to starve. Animals disappeared, and there were reports of cannibalism. Around 800,000 people died in the 900-day siege; that was around the same number of British and US deaths in World War II combined. Russia suffered the worst in terms of causalities, with nearly fourteen million deaths by the war's end.

Liberation of the USSR

While Hitler hoped to force Russia to surrender, he was met with stiff resistance. In October, he launched Operation Typhoon, which had the aim of capturing Moscow. However, the Soviets had gathered more troops and equipment. To make matters worse, the Russian roads became muddy and tricky to navigate during the fall months. This was known as Rasputitsa ("quagmire season") and was something the Soviets were used to managing. However, the Wehrmacht was quickly bogged down. While the Germans were delayed, the Soviets prepared to meet them. So, when the Germans finally got to Moscow, they were confronted by a strong Soviet Army.

During the brutal winter months, the German Army was finally forced to retreat. Operation Barbarossa had failed, partially because Hitler had failed to create supply lines that would strengthen his army while they fought in harsh and unfamiliar territory. The resilience of the Russians also played a large role. While the operation had weakened the Soviet Army, the brutal German tactics had made the Soviets determined to fight Germany until the bitter end. Instead of gaining a quick victory over a massive territory, Hitler had made a dangerous enemy.

In 1942, Hitler ordered another offensive against the USSR, which eventually failed. The Battle of Stalingrad, which took place from 1942 to 1943, even managed to turn the tide against Hitler. The siege of Leningrad wouldn't be lifted until early 1944. The Russians proved their resilience was stronger than Germany had anticipated.

The Allied powers eventually managed to overpower Hitler's army. In early 1945, Soviet troops invaded Poland and liberated Auschwitz. They found Nazi concentration camps and exposed the horrors perpetrated by Nazi Germany during the war. They were the first to reach Berlin, where a harsh battle took place between

Germans who still believed in the Nazi cause and the Soviet soldiers.

War Against Japan

Although Germany had been soundly defeated, the war wasn't over yet. In August 1945, the USSR declared war on Japan and invaded Japanese-occupied Manchuria (northeastern China). Two days prior, the Americans had dropped a nuclear bomb on Hiroshima with the goal of forcing Japan to surrender. However, the Japanese were deadlocked on what to do next. Some didn't believe the Americans would follow through on their promise to bomb another city. Some didn't even believe the US had bombed the city and wanted to send a fact-finding mission to discover the truth. The Japanese didn't have much time to do this, as the US had placed a deadline on Japan's unconditional surrender. In addition, the Japanese didn't account for the Soviet Army, as they believed the Soviets wouldn't be coordinated enough to attack them until the following year.

The USSR invaded Manchuria with a million troops, vastly outnumbering the Japanese army, which totaled about 700,000 soldiers. The invasion of Manchuria quickly proved to the Japanese that they would not be able to withstand sustained attacks from the Allies, and Emperor Hirohito began reconsidering the terms of his surrender. On August 9th, another atomic bomb was dropped on Nagasaki. About a week later, Emperor Hirohito announced Japan's surrender. On September 2nd, 1945, Japanese representatives signed the Instrument of Surrender, marking Japan's official surrender.

The Effects of the War

As soon as it became apparent that the war was going to end, Allied leaders met in Yalta to discuss what would happen after the war ended. The Germans had conquered many territories, and it was necessary to discuss what would happen to those territories once the Germans were defeated. British Prime Minister Winston Churchill advocated for democratic elections and democratic governments in Europe, especially in Poland. Meanwhile, Joseph Stalin wanted to create governments that were loyal to the USSR that would provide buffer zones in case Germany ever tried to attack the USSR again.

The Yalta Conference ruled that Poland would be ruled by a communist provisional government for a while and that Germany and Berlin would be occupied by America, Britain, the USSR, and France. In August 1945, the Allied powers met again in Potsdam, Germany. By then, US President Franklin D. Roosevelt had died. His successor, President Harry Truman, was suspicious of Stalin and his motives.

During the war, Stalin enacted a scorched-earth defensive policy, destroying anything that might have been used to assist the Germans. This meant parts of Russia needed to rebuild after the war. Stalin participated in many Allied conferences, including the Tehran Conference. He managed to maintain his alliance with Allied countries while expanding the Soviet Empire.

Allied leaders at the 1943 Tehran Conference.
https://commons.wikimedia.org/wiki/File:Allied_leaders_at_the_1943_Tehran_Conference.jpg

The Soviet Union occupied Romania, Bulgaria, Hungary, Poland, and Eastern Germany. During the war, the Soviets helped to set up communist dictatorships in many of the countries they occupied. In 1949, the Soviets set up the Communist German Democratic Republic in the Soviet-German occupation zone.

After the war ended, over a million Soviet soldiers remained stationed in Eastern Europe. In 1946, Winston Churchill said that it was as if an iron curtain had been dropped across the continent. Many people considered Churchill's words to be the first shot of the Cold War.

First Berlin Crisis of 1948

As the Cold War was brewing, the situation in Berlin worsened. Although Berlin was located in the Soviet occupation zone of Germany, it had also been divided between the other Allies. The western part of the city was controlled by the Allies, while the eastern part was controlled by the Soviets. It soon became apparent that both sides had very different visions for postwar Germany. The Soviets wanted to punish Germany by making the country pay steep reparations and used its industries to help the USSR recover from the war. The Allies wanted to help Germany recover from the war to help prevent the spread of communism.

In 1948, the Allies decided to combine their zones and create the state of Bizonia, a West German state with a stable currency. The Soviets opposed this plan and withdrew from the Allied Control Council, which had been created to coordinate the occupation of the zones. The Allied powers introduced a new currency called the Deutschmark, and the Soviets responded by releasing their own currency, the Ostmark. The Soviets also blocked all access to West Berlin. The blockade ensured the civilians of the western sector of the city were cut off from food, electricity, and other supplies. Two days later, a joint US and British relief operation was carried out. It was the largest air relief operation in history. Over two million tons of supplies were flown into West Berlin over eleven months.

The Soviets had hoped to cause the Allies to abandon West Berlin, but the relief mission prevented this from happening. The blockade was eventually lifted in 1949, but the division between East and West Berlin persisted.

The Cold War

By the end of the Second World War, the United States of America and the Soviet Union emerged as dominant world powers. However, they had diametrically opposed political ideologies. The Americans felt the Soviet policies were a threat that needed to be contained. Many US officials dedicated themselves to containing Soviet expansion, which was already taking place in Eastern Europe.

To that end, the Americans decided to use military force to contain communist expansion, which led to a massive increase in defense spending. During this time, the development of atomic bombs was increasing. In 1949, the USSR tested its atomic bomb, which led the US to develop the hydrogen bomb. The nature of these weapons increased the stakes of the Cold War to unprecedented heights.

The two countries became locked in a deadly arms race as they tried to outdo each other. When the first hydrogen bomb was tested in the Marshall Islands, it destroyed an island, resulted in a twenty-five-square-mile fireball, and blew a hole in the ocean floor. To make matters worse, these tests launched nuclear waste into the atmosphere. The Cold War ushered in the age of nuclear weapons, and it became alarmingly apparent what the consequences would be. Although the two engaged in proxy wars against each other, the two never engaged in an all-out war with each other.

Death of Stalin

After the war, Stalin continued his reign of terror, which included purges, exiles, and executions. He introduced the Soviets to the nuclear age and established numerous communist governments. In 1950, he allowed North Korea's communist leader, Kim Il Sung, to invade South Korea, the latter of which was supported by the US. This led to the Korean War.

Stalin may have been responsible for about twenty million deaths during his time in power, so it is no surprise that he became incredibly paranoid during his last years. He died in 1953 from a stroke. His body was embalmed and entombed in Lenin's Mausoleum in Moscow. In 1961, his body was removed and buried near the Kremlin. Stalin was succeeded by Nikita Khrushchev, who began the de-Stalinization process.

Warsaw Pact

In 1955, the US and other members of the North Atlantic Treaty Organization (NATO) decided to allow West Germany to become a part of NATO and remilitarize itself. The USSR viewed this as a direct threat to its power and responded with its own treaty. The Warsaw Pact was signed in Warsaw and included Poland, Albania, the USSR, Romania, East Germany, Bulgaria, Hungary, and Czechoslovakia. The treaty ensured that if any of the countries included in the treaty were attacked, then the other countries would have to defend the attacked country. Essentially, the Warsaw Pact set up a united military power that would be commanded by Marshal Ivan Konev of the USSR.

The Warsaw Pact lasted until 1991, but Albania left the pact after it turned to communist China for help when the Soviet leader, Nikita Khrushchev, deviated from Marxism. As non-communist governments rose in Eastern Europe in 1990, the Warsaw Pact became increasingly ineffective until it was finally dissolved.

Cuban Missile Crisis of 1962

In 1959, revolutionary leader Fidel Castro seized control of Cuba and allied himself with the USSR. In time, Cuba needed the Soviets to provide it with economic and military aid. In 1962, a US spy pilot photographed Soviet missiles in Cuba. US President John F. Kennedy responded by calling a group of advisors who formed the executive committee known as ExComm (Executive Committee of the National Security Council). Both the US and the USSR grappled with the diplomatic crisis, which could have easily ended in outright war.

For years, the Cold War had been stacked in favor of the West since they had nuclear weapons in Turkey and Western Europe. However, Cuba was alarmingly close to US territory, which meant the Soviets would be able to devastate the US more easily with their nuclear missiles.

The US launched the failed Bay of Pigs invasion, which prompted Castro and the USSR to find a way to deter another invasion. The Soviet presence in Cuba was unacceptable to the Americans, so they sent US vessels to block Soviet ships from approaching the island nation. It was a risky move since the Soviets could have breached the blockade, which would have surely led to war. Americans began stockpiling supplies as they feared the worse.

Thankfully, the Soviet ships didn't attempt to break the blockade. The standoff continued for a week while the two global superpowers communicated with each other. Both countries finally came to a deal. Khrushchev promised to remove his missiles from Cuba if the US promised not to invade Cuba and removed their missiles from Turkey. Both sides accepted the deal, and a nuclear war was averted.

Space Race

The Space Race, which was part of the Cold War, became an important area of competition between America and the USSR. Space had been dubbed the next frontier, and both countries were determined to prove their superiority in this new arena. In 1957, the Soviets launched Sputnik (meaning "traveling companion"), which was the first manmade object to be placed in Earth's orbit. The Soviets used an R-7 intercontinental ballistic missile to launch Sputnik, allowing the Russians to make inroads in space exploration. By doing so, the USSR showed off its military might to the rest of the world.

The Americans were surprised and displeased about this turn of events. The US was determined not to allow the USSR to gain too much ground in space exploration.

In 1958, the Americans launched Explorer I, their first satellite, which initiated the Space Race. US President Dwight D. Eisenhower created the National Aeronautics and Space Administration (NASA) that same year. In 1961, the Soviets launched the first man into space, which was another massive achievement. Despite the Soviets' many firsts in space, the Americans are thought to have won the Space Race in 1969 when Neil Armstrong became the first man to walk on the moon.

SALT Treaties and the Anti-Ballistic Missile Treaty

The Strategic Arms Limitation Talks were two conferences attended by the Americans and Soviets that resulted in international treaties. These conferences came to be known as SALT I and SALT II. The first round of negotiations began in 1969 in Helsinki, Finland. The Anti-Ballistic Missile Treaty was created (also referred to as the ABM Treaty). The ABM Treaty was an arms control treaty that aimed to reduce the production of more nuclear weapons and deter both countries from using weapons of mass destruction. The treaty ensured that both nations only had two missile complexes with only one hundred anti-ballistic missiles. The treaty would stay in place for three decades.

The second SALT conference took place from 1972 to 1979 and aimed to reduce the production of strategic nuclear weapons. This treaty banned new missile programs and limited both sides from developing new strategic missiles. The terms of this treaty would only last until 1985. Soon after the treaty was signed, the Soviets invaded Afghanistan, and the US chose not to ratify the terms of the agreement. However, both sides adhered to the treaty for a few more years.

In the meantime, the USSR was experiencing the de-Stalinization process. A few years after the SALT II treaty was negotiated, the USSR would officially dissolve.

Chapter 11: De-Stalinization to the Republic of Russia

Joseph Stalin was a brutal dictator who left his mark on the USSR. He helped turn his nation into a global superpower, but his methods also caused severe consequences for the Soviets. His successor, Nikita Khrushchev, was determined not to resort to the same methods and began a period of de-Stalinization, during which he worked to undo the cult of personality that had sprung up around Stalin.

While the USSR competed against the United States of America during the Cold War, the Soviet Union was going through several major changes and a period of stagnation. Eventually, the USSR would be dissolved, with the infamous Chernobyl (Chornobyl in Ukrainian) disaster playing a role in the downfall of the communist state. Russia would emerge as an independent republic, but the effects of privatization would lead to a fascinating new class in Russian society known as the oligarchs. This new period in Russian history would be led by two controversial figures: Boris Yeltsin and Vladimir Putin.

Nikita Khrushchev

Khrushchev was born in a small Russian village in 1894. When he was a teenager, he moved to the mining town of Yuzovka, where he worked as a metalworker. He joined the Bolsheviks in 1918 after their triumphant revolution. At the time, many idealistic youths joined the party since they believed communism was the answer to Russia's problems and wanted to be part of the new regime.

Khrushchev later moved to Moscow, where he rose to prominence within the communist government. He eventually became a part of Stalin's inner circle. Khrushchev managed to survive Stalin's paranoia and numerous political purges.

During the Second World War, he fought against Nazi Germany and helped rebuild the country after the war ended. He also earned merit when he suppressed nationalist uprisings in Ukraine. Six months after Stalin died, Khrushchev became the head of the Communist Party, which made him one of the most powerful people in the USSR.

Nikita Khrushchev.
https://commons.wikimedia.org/wiki/File:Nikita_Khruchchev_Colour.jpg

Khrushchev ruled the USSR with other officials under a collective leadership. At the time, Georgi Malenkov served as the premier of the USSR. In 1955, Malenkov was replaced by Nikolai Bulganin, one of Khrushchev's allies. In 1958, Khrushchev himself became the premier of the USSR.

De-Stalinization Policies

While Khrushchev had been one of Stalin's most dependable subordinates, he later criticized Stalin's policies, brutal tactics, egotistical acts, and lackluster leadership. In 1961, he moved Stalin's remains and renamed the city of Stalingrad Volgograd. These words and actions inspired protestors in Poland and Hungary to seek more autonomy. While the Polish were peacefully suppressed, the Hungarian rebellion was met with tanks and soldiers. In 1956, about 2,500 Hungarians were killed, while 13,000 were injured.

Khrushchev continued the de-Stalinization process and worked to undo the mythology around Stalin. He made official pronouncements to the Communist Party of the Soviet Union to remove some of the hyperbolic aspects of Stalin's legacy and blamed Stalin for terrorizing the party. Khrushchev enacted several policies that confirmed the importance of collective leadership, helped rehabilitate some who had been terrorized by Stalin, adopted more flexible foreign policies, and removed the threat of terror from everyday life. Soon, this process picked up the pace, and Stalin's name was removed from places that had been named after him, his writings were taken out of libraries, and his busts, statues, and portraits were all taken down. Intellectuals were given greater freedoms since censorship policies were relaxed.

Meanwhile, Khrushchev worked hard to improve agricultural production. He also weakened the secret police, let many political prisoners go, encouraged foreigners to visit the country, launched the space age, and eased censorship on artists. The Soviet space program has long been considered a great success.

Soviet Space Program

When the USSR launched Sputnik 1, it was the first manmade object to orbit Earth, but it wasn't widely celebrated. In fact, it wasn't announced to the Soviet public until the next day. Meanwhile, foreign countries took notice. Sputnik I had several interactive capabilities. Radio operators all over the world could dial into Sputnik I and listen to it beeping as it orbited Earth. Sputnik I was an amazing achievement that ushered in an interesting new age in human history.

1959 postage stamp depicting Laika.
https://commons.wikimedia.org/wiki/File:Posta_Romana_-_1959_-_Laika_120_B.jpg

Next, the Soviets tried to send animals to space. Laika, the first dog to be sent to space, was a stray taken from the streets of Moscow. She didn't survive the trip. Later, in 1960, the Soviets sent two female dogs, Belka and Strelka, who went to space but returned the next day safely.

The Soviets were the first to send a number of probes to the moon, and in 1966, Luna 9 arrived safely on the moon and took the first close-up pictures of the moon's surface. In 1961, the Soviets sent the first man to space. Yuri Gagarin circled Earth once in a Soviet spacecraft before he safely landed back on Earth. He became an overnight celebrity and was used to promote the space program. In 1963, the Soviets sent the first woman to space. Valentina Tereshkova spent three days in orbit and later became a cosmonaut engineer and influential government official. In 1965, Alexei Leonov became the first person to perform a spacewalk.

Eventually, the Soviets managed to put a rover on the moon. The Lunokhod 1 had eight wheels, four cameras, an X-ray spectrometer, and other fascinating gadgets. It transmitted from the moon's surface for about a year as it analyzed soil samples and sent pictures of the moon's surface back to the space program. After a year, it stopped transmitting. The Soviet space program remained active until the dissolution of the USSR.

Stagnation Era

Khrushchev had lofty plans for the USSR, and in 1961, he claimed the USSR was just twenty years away from achieving full communism. However, his popularity quickly dwindled, as it became clear his policies weren't working as well as they should have. Many people also felt that he mishandled the Cuban Missile Crisis.

In 1964, Khrushchev was deposed by his political rivals. He was succeeded by a collective leadership led by Leonid Brezhnev. The Soviet government focused on initiating several economic reforms that worked at first, which caused the USSR to flourish. However, inefficient Soviet bureaucracy and improper central planning led to a period of stagnation following the peak experienced in the early 1970s.

Several five-year plans were prioritized by economic planners in Moscow, who then came up with targets and quotas to be carried out by Soviet officials at local levels. However, this system had very little flexibility, which would prove to be disastrous. The boom in the Soviet economy that occurred from 1965 to the early 1970s caused the Soviet bureaucracy to grow very quickly. Soon, there were more bureaucrats and clerks than industrial workers. Besides that, the economy was becoming increasingly complex, which made it difficult to control.

The Soviet economy suffered from slow growth. For years, the Soviets had spent massive amounts on the military, and corruption became rampant. While the USSR boasted incredible technical and industrial growth, the agricultural sector became increasingly neglected. This resulted in disastrous consequences, as the USSR eventually wasn't producing enough grain to feed its people. This meant Moscow had to depend on foreign grain imports, which caused a notable trade deficit and impacted the USSR's reputation. The shortage of grain and consumer products caused a downfall in the standard of living. People were forced to wait for hours to buy basic items, while electrical items, cars, clothing, and footwear were rare. Products manufactured in the USSR were notoriously low quality, but products manufactured in the West were nearly impossible to obtain. The stagnation era severely weakened the USSR, leaving it unprepared for future difficulties.

Mikhail Gorbachev

Mikhail Gorbachev was born in 1931 in the North Caucasus region, which belonged to the Soviet Union. His family was poor, and he grew up during Stalin's reign. While he was still in school, he joined the Soviet political youth organization, where he was elected as the leader of his local group and later became a part of the district committee. When Gorbachev was old enough, he joined the Communist Party and went to Moscow State University, where he studied law. During his time at the university, he married a philosophy student named Raisa Titarenko. After he graduated, he began rising in the Communist Party's ranks.

During de-Stalinization under Khrushchev, Gorbachev enthusiastically supported Khrushchev's policies. He occupied several different positions within the government and saw firsthand the problems caused by the stagnation. Due to his upbringing as a peasant, he was also keenly aware of the hardships faced by the people of the Soviet Union. In 1985, he became the general secretary, which essentially made him the leader of the Soviet Union.

Mikhail Gorbachev.

The Official CTBTO Photostream, CC BY 2.0 <https://creativecommons.org/licenses/by/2.0>, via Wikimedia Commons; https://commons.wikimedia.org/wiki/File:Gorbachev_(cropped).png

While Gorbachev supported socialist ideals, he believed the Soviet Union needed extensive reformation. He introduced several policies, such as *glasnost* and *perestroika*. Gorbachev also initiated a few democratization policies and formed the Congress of People's Deputies, which would be made up of elected officials. This threatened the one-party state, and his policies angered strict Marxist-Leninist followers.

Perestroika and *Glasnost* Policies

As soon as Gorbachev came to power, he delivered a speech that highlighted the economic problems the Soviet Union was facing. He claimed the economic system was inefficient, making him the first Soviet leader to publicly criticize his own government. He also addressed these issues when he spoke to the Congress of the Communist Party. During this time, he advocated for extensive political and economic reforms or restructuring, which would be called *perestroika*. He also aimed to start a new age of transparency, which would be called *glasnost*.

Gorbachev proved true to his word and began systematically loosening the government's control over businesses, farms, and manufacturers. Individuals were freed from strict price controls, and many central committees within the government had their power curtailed. These policies encouraged businesses to work for profits. Gorbachev also allowed aspects of free-market capitalism into the Soviet Union, which allowed people to open stores, industries, and restaurants. These limited cooperative businesses would later form the basis of the oligarchical system, which is prevalent in modern-day Russia. Unfortunately, Gorbachev's reforms backfired, as the cost of food rose and workers began striking for higher wages. To make matters worse, he faced backlash from within the Communist Party, as many felt he was betraying communist ideals. More liberal parties accused him of not making enough changes.

Besides reforming the economy, Gorbachev also worked on restructuring the political system. In 1988, he set plans in motion to hold the first democratic elections in Russia since 1917. This allowed many officials to campaign for a place in the new Congress of People's Deputies. Thanks to *glasnost*, many censorship rules were lifted, which allowed the press to honestly report the campaigns. In 1990, Gorbachev became the first president of the

USSR. He also withdrew Soviet troops from Afghanistan and began engaging with Western leaders, most notably US President Ronald Reagan.

While Gorbachev had held high hopes for the restructuring of the Soviet government, his policies ultimately failed and led to the swift end of the Soviet Union.

Chernobyl Disaster

After the Second World War, the USSR began heavily investing in nuclear power and weapons, which is evidenced by the events of the Cold War. In 1977, Soviet scientists installed nuclear reactors at a power plant in Chernobyl (Chornobyl), Ukraine. A few years later, in 1986, workers conducted a test to see if the reactor would be cooled if the plant somehow lost power. Unfortunately, the workers disregarded several safety protocols, which caused a power surge. The workers tried to shut down the reactor, but it was too late, as another power surge set off a series of explosions that exposed the nuclear core and released radioactive materials into the environment. Firefighters tried to kill the fires and contain the contamination. Chernobyl and Pripyat (a nearby city that housed the people who worked at the plant) were only evacuated about thirty-six hours after the explosion.

The Soviet government attempted to cover up the disaster, but the radiation had spread as far as Sweden, which forced the Soviet government to make an announcement about the disaster. The disaster released 30 percent of Chernobyl's uranium into the atmosphere, and the Soviets had to evacuate 335,000 people from a 19-mile radius around the reactor. This area came to be known as the exclusion zone. About twenty-eight people died in the accident, while one hundred were injured.

The disaster contributed to the end of the Soviet Union and kicked off the global anti-nuclear movement.

Fall of the Berlin Wall

In 1961, the communist government of East Germany built a massive wall to separate East and West Berlin. The official purpose of the wall was to keep Western fascists from entering East Berlin, but the truth was that many people were defecting from East Berlin to West Berlin. The wall kept the people contained. Before the wall, citizens were allowed to move freely between the two sides of the city, but the wall put a stop to that. Few people were allowed to cross the wall. The wall separated families and prevented refugees from fleeing East Germany.

In 1989, a spokesperson for East Berlin's Communist Party announced that people were free to cross the border. About two million people from East Berlin visited the western part of the city, resulting in a massive street party. Soon, people grabbed hammers and picks to tear down pieces of the wall. Cranes and bulldozers began removing sections of the Berlin Wall until it finally came down. In 1990, East and West Germany were reunified.

Dissolution of the USSR

Gorbachev aimed to improve the Soviet Union's relationship with the rest of the world, as he hoped this could help the Soviet economy. He bowed out of the arms race, despite the fact US President Ronald Reagan had initiated a massive military buildup. He also reduced Soviet troops in Eastern Europe and withdrew his troops from the controversial war in Afghanistan. In 1989, a revolution took place in Poland, where non-communist trade unionists successfully negotiated for free elections. This sparked more revolutions in Eastern Europe. Czechoslovakia overthrew its communist government, and countries within the Soviet Union began declaring their independence from Russia.

Gorbachev's efforts to bring an end to the Cold War earned him the Nobel Peace Prize in 1990. In 1991, Gorbachev was placed under house arrest by members of the Communist Party. The coup seemed successful, and a state of emergency was declared.

The military attempted to take Moscow, but Russian citizens formed barricades and human chains to stop the tanks and protect the Russian Parliament. Boris Yeltsin, who was the chair of Parliament, supported the civilians' efforts. In the end, the coup failed. Yeltsin famously stood on top of a tank in front of Parliament to stop the military from advancing. In December, Belarus broke away from the USSR. Eight other countries followed, with many more having already broken away, such as Ukraine and Armenia. Yeltsin took control of the KGB (the USSR's security agency) and Parliament, and on December 25th, 1991, Gorbachev resigned as president. The USSR had officially fallen.

Boris Yeltsin

Boris Yeltsin was born in 1931 in the Ural Mountains. His family was poor, as his peasant grandparents had been uprooted during Stalin's rule. His father had been sent to the Gulag. In 1949, Yeltsin attended the Urals Polytechnic Institute. He became a civil engineer and married Naina Iosifovna Girina. In 1961, he joined the Communist Party and quickly rose within the government. Yeltsin was summoned to Moscow by Gorbachev and fought against corruption within the government. However, in 1987, he lost his position after he clashed with Gorbachev. In 1990, Yeltsin became the chair of the Russian Parliament and left the Communist Party. In 1991, he was elected as the Russian president.

Boris Yeltsin.

Yeltsin immediately began dismantling the Soviet Union and the Communist Party. He took away many price controls and privatized major state assets. Yeltsin also adopted many free-market principles, allowing the stock exchange, private banks, and commodities exchanges to come into existence. This led to increased inflation and a high cost of living. A select few oligarchs were able to take control of privatized state assets and became incredibly wealthy in a short amount of time. Unfortunately, corruption, crime, and decreased industrial output became rampant. Yeltsin allowed Western culture into Russia, supported the freedom of the press, agreed to nuclear arms reductions, and withdrew soldiers from Eastern Europe.

In 1999, Yeltsin surprised the world when he resigned from his post and asked for forgiveness for his past mistakes. He then gave power to his successor, Vladimir Putin.

First and Second Chechen Wars

The First Chechen War was a war of independence fought by the Chechen Republic of Ichkeria against Russia. It took place from 1994 to 1996. The war was in response to the Russian attempt to secretly overthrow the Ichkerian government. While the Russians had the advantage in regard to firepower, military technology, weapons, and soldiers, they found the Chechen guerillas difficult to defeat. The Russian military was demoralized since it was not making much progress, and the Russian public firmly opposed the war. Yeltsin's government was forced to declare a ceasefire in 1996, which resulted in a peace treaty in 1997.

The Second Chechen War took place from 1999 to 2009. In 1999, Islamic soldiers took over Russia's Dagestan region and declared it to be an independent state. By 2009, the Russians had largely brought an end to the fighting. The Russians left Chechnya, and the local police were tasked with dealing with any minor insurgencies. The exiled leader of the separatist government eventually called for an end to the resistance, bringing the conflict to a stop.

Vladimir Putin

Vladimir Putin was born in 1952 in Leningrad (now St. Petersburg). He attended Leningrad State University, where he studied law. After he graduated, he became a foreign intelligence officer for the KGB. In 1991, he retired from the KGB, and in 1994, he became the first deputy chairman of St. Petersburg. In 1996, he moved to Moscow and moved up within the government. Putin gained a reputation for being able to get things done. In 1998, he became the director of the FSB (the Federal Security Service, the

KGB's successor). Finally, in 1999, Putin was chosen as Yeltsin's successor and became president. Putin proved to be a levelheaded leader who launched a successful operation against the rebels in Chechnya.

Putin helped the economy recover, a feat that was aided by the rise of oil prices. He encouraged economic growth, which improved his popularity with the Russian government. In 2008, he was forced to step down from his position due to a constitutional provision. He chose Dmitry Medvedev as his successor, and he was appointed as prime minister. Although Medvedev held the position of president, Putin was still the one calling the shots. In 2012, Putin was reelected as president, and he made Medvedev his prime minister. While Putin faced a lot of opposition, he managed to stifle protest movements and had opposition leaders put in prison.

Vladimir Putin.

During Putin's third term as president, Russia annexed Crimea and later sponsored a war in eastern Ukraine. These actions led to international sanctions that caused a financial crisis in Russia. During his fourth term as president, he ordered a military buildup on the border of Ukraine and then accused the Ukraine government of persecuting its Russian-speaking minority (although history might tell a different tale later on, at the moment, it is believed these are false accusations). Putin ordered an invasion of Ukraine in 2022, which led to increased sanctions and international condemnation. Many have called for Putin to be prosecuted on charges of war crimes.

Chapter 12: Russian Arts, Literature, and Science

During Russia's long and storied history, its art and culture went through several significant changes. The climactic events that took place in the country's history provided inspiration for some of the most influential literature and music in the world. At various periods in Russia's history, the country housed cities that became intellectual hubs, attracting scholars from all over the world. This led to major advancements in subjects like science and mathematics.

This chapter explores the lives and achievements of some of Russia's most talented and influential musicians, writers, and scientists. These individuals provide a unique view into the different time periods in which they lived.

The Great Russian Musicians

- Tchaikovsky

Pyotr Ilyich Tchaikovsky was born in 1840 in Kamsko-Votkinsk, Russia. He was the second of six children, and his father was the manager of a metalworking company. Early in his childhood, Tchaikovsky displayed an interest in music and wrote his first song at four years old. In 1845, he began taking piano lessons and studied the works of Chopin and Friedrich Kalkbrenner. At the time, music wasn't taught in Russian schools, so Tchaikovsky's parents arranged a career in civil service. In 1850, he attended the Imperial School of Jurisprudence in St. Petersburg. He was a popular student who got good grades. Around this time, he formed intense emotional bonds with several of his peers.

Pyotr Ilyich Tchaikovsky, c. 1870.
https://commons.wikimedia.org/wiki/File:Pyotr_Tchaikovsky_%D1%81._1870.jpg

As a teenager, Tchaikovsky's father invited a professional teacher to give Tchaikovsky lessons. He was heavily influenced by Italian singing teacher Luigi Piccioli, which led to a passion for Italian music. In 1861, he traveled to Germany, France, and England. He later attended the newly founded Russian Musical Society. In 1865, Johann Strauss the Younger conducted Tchaikovsky's Characteristic Dances in Pavlovsk. This would be the first time his work was played in public. While working as a teacher for the Russian Musical Society (later the Moscow Conservatory), he produced his first opera, *The Voyevoda*, and his first symphony, Symphony No. 1 in G Minor.

In time, his music became increasingly popular throughout Russia and the world. Tchaikovsky became known for his colorful orchestration and impressive harmonies. He eventually wrote seven symphonies, three ballets, five suites, three piano concertos, a violin concerto, eleven overtures, four cantatas, three string quartets, a string sextet, twenty choral works, and over one hundred songs. According to tradition, he died in 1893 from complications arising from cholera. However, some speculate that he committed suicide.

While Tchaikovsky experienced major criticism during his lifetime, he became a national icon in the Soviet Union. He experienced a lot of criticism because Russians didn't see it as being "national" enough and too European. Although Russia denies that Tchaikovsky was gay, his biographers all agree that he was but that he kept it private for most of his life. Tchaikovsky's letters are definite proof of his sexual orientation, as he wrote about being enamored with his servant and his nephew.

• Rachmaninoff

Sergei Rachmaninoff was born in 1873 on his grandparents' estate in the Novgorod district. His father was an army officer, and it was assumed Rachmaninoff would also join the army, but his father lost the family fortune and abandoned his family. Rachmaninoff's cousin, Alexander Siloti, who was a pianist and conductor, noticed the boy's talents and arranged for him to study music in Moscow. Rachmaninoff was tutored by Nikolai Zverev and later attended the Moscow Conservatory.

After Rachmaninoff graduated from the conservatory, he won a gold medal for his opera *Aleko,* which was based on one of Pushkin's poems. His two compositions, Prelude in C-sharp Minor and Piano Concerto No. 2 in C Minor, launched him into stardom. The young musician suffered from bouts of self-doubt and depression but was helped by the psychiatrist Nikolai Dahl, who reportedly helped Rachmaninoff regain his confidence. In 1905, Rachmaninoff worked at the Bolshoi Theatre and saw firsthand the events of the 1905 Revolution.

Later, he moved with his family to Dresden, where he wrote three major scores. He conducted several musical tours in the United States, which were successful. Rachmaninoff was invited to work at the Boston Symphony but declined in favor of returning to Russia.

After the Russian Revolution, Rachmaninoff went into self-imposed exile and spent time between the US and Switzerland. His alienation from his home country had a severe negative impact on his creative ability. He lived a rather isolated life from then on and wrote a few more pieces before his death in 1943.

- **Rimsky-Korsakov**

Nikolai Rimsky-Korsakov was born near Novgorod in 1844 to an aristocratic family. He showed an affinity for music at an early age but was sent to study at the Russian Imperial Naval College in St. Petersburg, after which he joined the Russian Navy. While Rimsky-Korsakov was in the navy, he completed his first symphony, which made him the first Russian to compose one. He completed two more works before he resigned from the navy in 1873. Rimsky-Korsakov worked with a group of composers who often collaborated and edited each other's work. The group came to be known as "The Five."

Rimsky-Korsakov was largely self-taught but became a professor of composition and orchestration at the St. Petersburg Conservatory. He produced many orchestral works and influenced later composers. In 1905, Rimsky-Korsakov was fired from the conservatory due to his political views but was eventually reinstated once a few of his colleagues resigned in protest. His opera *The Golden Cockerel* harshly criticized imperial Russia and was banned. He died in 1908 and was interred in St. Petersburg.

- **Stravinsky**

Igor Stravinsky was born in 1882 near St. Petersburg. His father worked as a bass singer at the Mariinsky Theatre in St. Petersburg. Later, Stravinsky studied law but switched to composition. Rimsky-Korsakov was the head of the Russian Conservatory at the time and offered to give Stravinsky private lessons, which Stravinsky eagerly accepted.

During the First World War, Stravinsky moved to Switzerland and later to Paris, where he wrote ballets and other compositions. He loved exploring different aspects of art and literature. Stravinsky notably worked with Sergei Diaghilev, Pablo Picasso, Jean Cocteau, and George Balanchine.

Igor Stravinsky.

Stravinsky was known for his innovative ballets that revolutionized the genre. His musical works ranged from opera to jazz, and he experimented with many different classical forms of music. Stravinsky was an accomplished pianist and conductor. He also worked as a writer and complied the *Poetics of Music*. Stravinsky moved to the US in 1939. He became a naturalized US citizen and remained there until he died in 1971.

- **Shostakovich**

Dmitri Shostakovich was born in 1906 in St. Petersburg. Shostakovich displayed remarkable musical talent after he began taking piano lessons at the age of nine. In 1918, he wrote a funeral march and was admitted to the Petrograd Conservatory a year later. Shostakovich made his musical debut in 1926 with the Leningrad Philharmonic Orchestra, which performed his first symphony. It was well received, and the crowd demanded an encore.

Shostakovich was reportedly an obsessive man who was obsessed with cleanliness and regularly sent himself mail to check that the postal service was still working. His peers said he was vulnerable and receptive, which likely increased the quality of his music.

He achieved fame in the Soviet Union, but some of his work, particularly his opera *Lady Macbeth of Mtsensk*, was condemned by the government. He suffered from state censure, and his work was occasionally checked by the state.

His work was often characterized by distinct contrasts, neoclassical influences, and elements of the grotesque. During the Second World War, he composed Symphony No. 7, which was written during the siege of Leningrad. The composition would come to be known as his most famous wartime composition.

Shostakovich loved using different musical techniques, making his work varied and interesting. The composer was greatly influenced by Stravinsky's works. He also wrote a lot of music for films and the theater. Scholars continue to debate his work, especially the nature of his work and his feelings toward the Soviet government. He is widely regarded as a musical genius. Shostakovich died of heart failure in 1975 in Moscow.

Famous Russian Writers

- ## Leo Tolstoy

Leo Tolstoy was born in 1828 on his family's estate in the Tula Province of Russia. He was the youngest of four and was raised by his father's cousin when his mother died. During his childhood, he lost several close family members but always remembered his childhood fondly.

Tolstoy was educated at home by French and German tutors. In 1843, he attended the University of Kazan, where he studied Oriental languages. He wasn't a successful student and was forced to transfer to a law program. He partied excessively and eventually left university without a degree.

In 1847, Tolstoy returned to his parent's estate, where he attempted to become a farmer, but his work was interrupted by his frequent social visits to Moscow and Tula. During this time, he began keeping a journal, which would help develop his writing skills.

Leo Tolstoy.

He later joined the army, and in 1855, he fought in the Crimean War. During his time in the army, Tolstoy began working on a story called *Childhood*. It would become his first published work. He then began working on a book called *The Cossacks*, which detailed daily life in the army. It was finished after he left the military.

When Tolstoy returned to Russia, he found his works had made an impact on Russian literary circles. He refused to ally himself with any particular school of thought and declared himself an anarchist. He went to Paris for a while but eventually returned to Russia. In 1862, he married Sophia Andreyevna Bers. In the 1860s, Tolstoy spent his time creating one of his great works, *War and Peace*. It was well received, and in 1873, he began working on *Anna Karenina*, which also achieved critical and public acclaim.

Later in life, Tolstoy suffered from depression caused by a spiritual crisis. He attempted to find the answers he sought in the Russian Orthodox Church but wasn't satisfied with what he found. He then decided to develop his own beliefs, which caused the Russian Orthodox Church to oust him from the church. During the last years of his life, he regarded himself as a religious leader and was influenced by the teachings of Mahatma Gandhi. Tolstoy eventually died in 1910.

- **Alexander Pushkin**

Alexander Pushkin was born in 1799 and later became Russia's most famous poet. He was born into a prestigious noble family; many of his ancestors had played influential roles in Russian history. He became a student at the Lyceum of Tsarskoe Selo and became enamored with French poetry and Russian neoclassicism. He graduated in 1817 and became involved in partying and politics.

Pushkin's early poems often commented on autocracy's limits and would later be used by the Decembrists, a military organization that challenged Tsar Nicholas I. He was known for breaking poetry traditions, and his mock epic, *Ruslan and Ludmila*, was a massive success. However, his political views got him exiled to southern Russia. During this time, he traveled extensively, writing lyrics and poems.

Alexander Pushkin.
https://commons.wikimedia.org/wiki/File:AleksandrPushkin.jpg

Pushkin later invented a new stanza in his poem *Eugene Onegin*. He was eventually released from his exile but was subject to government censure.

His life was defined by romantic and political scandals that put a strain on his position in the royal court. In 1831, he married Natalia Goncharova. She was a famous beauty who enjoyed a good position at court. Nicholas I was infatuated with Natalia. A French royalist, Georges-Charles de Heeckeren d'Anthès, also pursued her, which caused Pushkin to challenge him to a duel. Pushkin lost the duel and died from his injuries about two days later.

Pushkin left a lasting legacy on Russian literature, and the Russian public mourned his passing.

• Fyodor Dostoyevsky

Fyodor Dostoevsky was born in 1821 and was the second of seven children. His father was a retired military surgeon who worked at the Mariinsky Hospital for the Poor in Moscow, which was located in one of the worst areas in the city. Dostoevsky grew up among the poor and developed a deep compassion for them, which would become evident in his later works.

As a child, Dostoevsky loved spending time with the patients in his father's hospital since they would regale him with their stories. In 1837, he was sent to the Military Engineering Academy in St. Petersburg. Dostoevsky suffered from epilepsy from the age of nine; some of his characters are also afflicted with the condition.

In 1844, Dostoevsky began writing fiction after he left the army. His first short novel, *Poor Folk*, was met with great acclaim. In 1849, he was arrested for being part of a liberal intellectual group. He was sentenced to death, which was later commuted to four years of exile with hard labor in a Siberian labor camp.

When Dostoevsky returned to St. Petersburg, he began a successful literary journal with his brother. His wife and brother died in quick succession, which plunged him into a deep depression. He began gambling and accumulated massive debts. Many claim that his best-known novel, *Crime and Punishment*, was completed in a hurry because he needed an advance from his publisher.

Dostoevsky has been accredited with founding existentialism and showed an acute understating of human psychology. He also managed to capture Russia's political, social, and spiritual state on paper while making his work compelling. He is known as one of the greatest writers of all time and influenced many other famous writers, such as Ernest Hemingway. He died in 1881 after suffering from multiple pulmonary hemorrhages.

- **Maxim Gorky**

Aleksey Peshkov was born in 1868 in Novgorod. He later adopted the pseudonym Maxim Gorky. His father was a shipping agent who died when Gorky was five. He was then sent to live with his grandparents. He went to school until he was eight years old before he was sent out to earn his living. He worked as an errand boy, a dishwasher, and an assistant. Gorky was introduced to reading at a young age, and it soon became his passion.

Gorky was frequently beaten by his employers and treated terribly by his grandfather. These experiences made him intimately aware of the problems faced by the Russian working class. He claimed his childhood experiences were often bitter, which was why he chose the word *gorky* (meaning "bitter") as his pseudonym. He attempted suicide as a young man but survived and became a tramp.

Maxim Gorky.
https://commons.wikimedia.org/wiki/File:Maxim_Gorky_LOC_Restored_edit1.jpg

In 1895, his story "Chelkash" was published and met with critical acclaim, launching his career. His works were compared to Leo Tolstoy and Anton Chekhov. Gorky wrote a series of novels and plays that weren't as well received as his previous work. He later became a Marxist and supported the Social Democratic Party.

When the Bolsheviks began rising to prominence, he found himself at odds with Lenin but gave much of his earnings to the party, which became one of the Bolsheviks' main sources of income. In 1906, he left Russia and lived in Italy. While Gorky agreed with some of the Bolsheviks' policies, he opposed their seizure of power in 1917. He tried to help exiled and imprisoned writers but was opposed by Lenin, who exiled him in 1921.

During his last few years, he produced some of his greatest works. Gorky died suddenly in 1936 while receiving medical treatment. Many speculated that he was covertly killed by Stalin since he was openly critical of Stalin's government. The theory has some merit, as Stalin famously didn't take criticism well.

• Nikolai Gogol

Nikolai Gogol was born in 1809 in Ukraine, which at the time was part of the Russian Empire. His works later became some of the most beloved pieces of Russian literature. He has been called the first Russian realist, as he often used comic realism and satire to great effect. His work influenced other Russian writers, namely Ivan Turgenev, Leo Tolstoy, and Fyodor Dostoyevsky.

Gogol was born into a noble family, and his father died when he was still a teenager. His mother raised him as a Christian, which would later influence many of his decisions. In 1828, Gogol moved to St. Petersburg, where he became friends with Pushkin, who greatly supported his career. Many of his witty lines later became popular Russian sayings. His work was well received, and he worked as a history professor at St. Petersburg University.

His play, *The Inspector General* (also known as *The Government Inspector*), was a biting satire of Russian bureaucracy. It caused so much controversy that Gogol decided to spend the next twelve years abroad. He found ways past political censorship by using fantastical and supernatural elements to soften anything that offended the government. His work later inspired other Soviet writers to use the same methods.

Gogol died in 1852 after burning the manuscript of his last book since he was unable to reconcile his Christian beliefs to his writings. He died a few days later after taking to his bed and refusing to take any food.

• Anton Chekhov

Anton Chekhov was born in 1860 in Taganrog, Russia. He attended a local school for Greek boys. In 1879, he moved to Moscow, where he enrolled at a university and studied medicine. His father had been unable to work for years at that point, so Chekhov became the family's breadwinner. He worked for a time as a journalist and comic writer, which he used to support his family and pay for medical school. In 1888, Chekhov was already a popular writer with the general public. Eventually, he strayed away from his comedic writing and began focusing on serious writing that studied misery and despair.

Anton Chekhov in 1904.
https://commons.wikimedia.org/wiki/File:Anton_Chekhov_1904.JPG

Chekhov's works became renowned for exposing human nature, while his plays and short stories often lacked clean solutions. His work created a unique atmosphere and was often described as haunting. He was able to describe Russian life simply without relying on literary devices.

Chekhov remained popular in Russia for most of his life but only received international attention after the First World War. Anton Chekhov died in 1904 after a long battle with tuberculosis.

- **Aleksandr Solzhenitsyn**

Aleksandr Solzhenitsyn was born in Russia in 1918 to a family who opposed the Soviet anti-religious campaign and clung to their Russian Orthodox faith. As a child, he became an atheist and Marxist-Leninist. He served as a captain in the Soviet Army during the Second World War. However, he was sentenced to eight years in the Gulag for criticizing Joseph Stalin in one of his private letters.

Due to his time in the camps, he became an Eastern Orthodox Christian. After Solzhenitsyn was released from the Gulag, he began writing novels about his experiences and the Soviet Union's repression. His first novel was published in 1862 with Nikita Khrushchev's approval; it provided a detailed account of Stalin's oppression. In 1963, Solzhenitsyn published a book called *Matryona's Place*, which would be the last book he published in the Soviet Union.

Once Khrushchev was removed from power, the Soviet government discouraged Solzhenitsyn from writing any more novels. He kept working but published his books in other countries. His works angered the Soviet government. In 1974, he lost his Soviet citizenship and was flown to West Germany. Two years later, he moved to the United States, where he continued writing. During this time, he harshly criticized communism and tried to raise awareness about the repression caused by the Soviet Union. He regained his citizenship after the USSR was dissolved and lived in Russia until he died in 2008.

Influential Russian Scientists

- **Dimitri Mendeleev**

Dmitri Mendeleev was born in 1834 in Siberia. His father was a school principal and a teacher. Mendeleev was raised as an Orthodox Christian and encouraged to search for scientific and divine truths. He had seventeen siblings, fourteen of whom survived childhood. Mendeleev was the youngest.

In 1850, he entered the Main Pedagogical Institute in St. Petersburg. In 1861, he published a textbook on organic chemistry, which won him the Demidov Prize from the Petersburg Academy of Sciences. In 1864, he became a professor at the Saint Petersburg Technological Institute, and a year later, he taught at Saint Petersburg State University. Mendeleev managed to turn St. Petersburg into an internationally recognized center focused on chemistry research.

Dimitri Mendeleev.

In 1863, there were about fifty-six known chemical elements, but chemists were discovering new elements almost every year. This caused a dilemma, with chemists trying to organize these elements differently. Mendeleev's textbook, the *Principles of Chemistry*, became one of the most influential textbooks of his time. While working on the textbook, he tried to arrange the elements according to their chemical properties. He soon noticed patterns, which led him to create the periodic table of elements. Mendeleev later published his periodic table in a journal and even predicted a few new elements.

Today, Mendeleev is known as the "Father of the Periodic Table." Although his periodic table was by no means finished, it left room for discoveries and improvements. Mendeleev died in 1907 of the flu.

- ## Mikhail Lomonosov

Mikhail Lomonosov was born in 1711 in the village of Denisovka, which would later be renamed in his honor. He was born to a poor family and eventually made his way to Moscow on foot. Lomonosov had a boundless curiosity and thirst for knowledge that wasn't being satisfied in his rural village, which made him decide to seek education elsewhere. He was able to gain admission into the Slavic Greek Latin Academy, where he made rapid progress.

In 1734, he was sent to St. Petersburg, where he distinguished himself and was sent to complete his education in a foreign country. He went to the University of Marburg in Hesse, Germany, which was one of the most important universities in Europe. There, he studied under the influential German Enlightenment philosopher Christian Wolff. During this time, he also began writing poetry.

When Lomonosov returned to Russia, he quickly rose to prominence and was made a professor of chemistry at St. Petersburg State University. He helped found Moscow State University and eventually became the secretary of state. He made many scientific discoveries and greatly improved Russian education.

Lomonosov was also the first person to ever record the freezing of mercury. In 1745, he published a comprehensive catalog of over three thousand minerals, and a few years later, he was able to explain the formation of icebergs.

He had many varied interests, which included the ancient art of mosaics. He even set up a glass factory that produced the first non-Italian stained-glass mosaics. Lomonosov made about forty great mosaics. He also reformed the Russian literary language and wrote extensively about literary theories. Lomonosov was deeply interested in poetry, and his work is considered the best of his generation.

Lomonosov died in St. Petersburg in 1765 and left behind a legacy as a gifted polymath and writer who revolutionized Russian literature, science, and education. Due to his efforts, he is one of the most well-known and influential scientists and writers in Russian history.

• Ivan Pavlov

Ivan Pavlov was born in Russia in 1849. His father was a priest, so Ivan was educated at a church school and theological seminary. However, he was introduced to the works of I. M. Sechenov and Charles Darwin, which led him to pursue a scientific career instead. He studied chemistry and physiology at St. Petersburg University. He later went on to study under Rudolf Heidenhain and Carl Ludwig, who were some of the most renowned physiologists of the time.

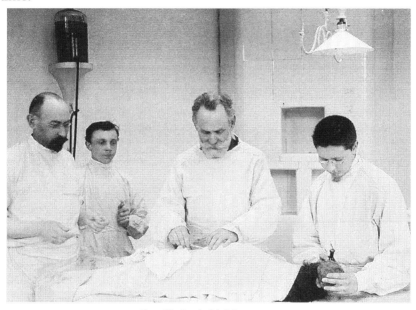

Ivan Pavlov in his laboratory.

Pavlov studied human digestion extensively and gained a deep understanding of gastric secretions and the role of the mind and body in the digestive process. In 1897, he published a book called *Lectures on the Work of the Digestive Glands.* His work earned him a Nobel Prize for Physiology in 1904. He also received an honorary doctorate from Cambridge University and the Order of the Legion of Honor.

Pavlov is best known for his research on conditioned reflexes. He was able to prove that dogs instinctively salivated at the prospect of food. Later, he realized the dogs began salivating at the mere sight of a person in a lab coat since those people usually brought the dogs food. They learned the lab coat usually resulted in food, which triggered an unconditioned response. From then on, Pavlov began to study conditioning. He discovered that certain stimuli could cause dogs to associate those stimuli with food, triggering a conditioned response. Pavlov also found out how to break that response.

While he tested his theories on animals, the principles could also be applied to humans. Pavlov believed that certain behaviors in people with psychological problems were conditioned responses that could be unlearned. His theories would later be confirmed.

Pavlov continued working in his lab until he died in 1936 in Leningrad after contracting double pneumonia. His lab was turned into a museum, and a monument was erected in his honor.

Conclusion

Russia is the largest country in the world and has a long and varied history. While this book doesn't contain every event from Russia's history, it includes some of the most important periods, incidents, and individuals.

The first section of this book dealt with the early Slavic kingdoms, the Mongol invasion, and Russia's time as part of the Golden Horde. These events left a lasting mark on Russia. At one point in Russia's history, the Slavs were ruled by Viking princes who built a powerful state. The Mongols wreaked havoc on Russia, but eventually, Russian princes were able to overthrow their Mongol overlords to build a strong ruling dynasty.

The second section of this book explored the Christianization of the Rus' and the rise of the Russian Empire, which all started with the Grand Duchy of Moscow. Eventually, the Rurikid dynasty was replaced by the Romanovs after a long period of political and economic strife. The Romanovs held onto power for a little over three centuries. During that time, several influential leaders took the throne, including Peter the Great and Catherine the Great. While they held on to their absolute autocracy, they managed to reform and modernize the country. Their efforts helped build the mighty Russian Empire, which was divided between Slavophiles and Westernizers. Both sides thought they knew what was best for Russia. Imperial Russia managed to defeat Napoleon but was severely weakened by the Crimean War. As the ideas of revolution became prevalent in Russia, Tsar Alexander II tried to reform his country to meet some of the demands made by revolutionists. Unfortunately, that work was undone by his successor, Tsar Alexander III, who was a firm Slavophile.

In the third section, the events of World War I and the Russian Revolution were discussed. The Romanovs were overthrown, and the monarchy was substituted with the world's first communist government under Lenin, who formed the USSR.

Finally, this book looked at the rule of Stalin, Russia's involvement in World War II, and the start of the Cold War. During this period, Russia belonged to the Soviet Union and boasted an impressive collection of nuclear weapons and a flourishing space program. However, the USSR went through a period of stagnation, which severely weakened it. The USSR wouldn't survive for much longer. When it was dissolved, its state assets were privatized.

Russian history is full of interesting events and fascinating figures who either made Russia better or worse. Comprehensive knowledge of Russian history will contribute to an expanded understanding of world history and current events. Russia is certainly making news in the headlines as of this writing, and it is likely that trend will continue in the future.

Here's another book by Enthralling History that you might like

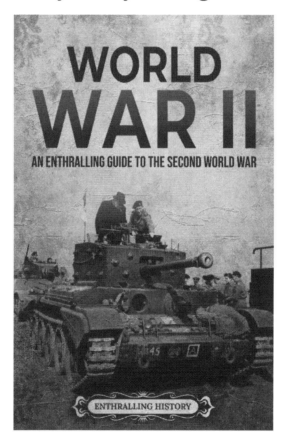

Free limited time bonus

Stop for a moment. We have a free bonus set up for you. The problem is this: we forget 90% of everything that we read after 7 days. Crazy fact, right? Here's the solution: we've created a printable, 1-page pdf summary for this book that you're reading now. All you have to do to get your free pdf summary is to go to the following website: **https://livetolearn.lpages.co/enthrallinghistory/**

Once you do, it will be intuitive. Enjoy, and thank you!

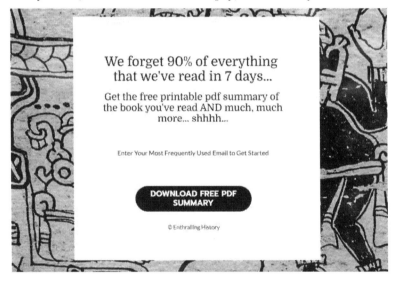

Bibliography

- Title: Russia: A Timeline

Date Accessed: 11/8/2022

Link: https://www.history.com/topics/russia/russia-timeline

- Title: Slavs and the Early Slav Culture

Date Accessed: 11/8/2022

Link: https://www.encyclopedia.com/humanities/encyclopedias-almanacs-transcripts-and-maps/slavs-and-early-slav-culture

- Title: Slavs

Date Accessed: 11/8/2022

Link: https://www.worldhistory.org/Slavs/

- Title: When Viking Kings and Queens Ruled Medieval Russia

Date Accessed: 11/8/2022

Link: https://www.history.com/news/vikings-in-russia-kiev-rus-varangians-prince-oleg

- Title: Kievan Rus'

Date Accessed: 11/8/2022

Link: https://www.worldhistory.org/Kievan_Rus/

- Title: Khazars

Date Accessed: 11/8/2022

Link: https://cs.mcgill.ca/~rwest/wikispeedia/wpcd/wp/k/Khazars.htm

- Title: The Rise and Fall of Kievan Rus'

Date Accessed: 11/8/2022

Link: https://www.themaparchive.com/the-rise-and-fall-of-kievan-rus/

- Title: Olga of Kiev: One Saint You Do Not Want to Mess With

Date Accessed: 11/8/2022

Link: https://www.historyanswers.co.uk/medieval-renaissance/olga-of-kiev-one-saint-you-do-not-want-to-mess-with/

- Title: The Great Migration and Early Slavic History

Date Accessed: 11/8/2022

Link: https://about-history.com/the-great-migration-and-early-slavic-history/

- Title: The Slavs and Byzantium

Date Accessed: 11/8/2022

Link: https://unesdoc.unesco.org/ark:/48223/pf0000046109

- Title: Vladimir I and Christianization

Date Accessed: 12/8/2022

Link: https://courses.lumenlearning.com/atd-herkimer-westerncivilization/chapter/vladimir-i-and-christianization/

- Title: Eastern Orthodox Church

Date Accessed: 12/8/2022

Link: https://www.bbc.co.uk/religion/religions/christianity/subdivisions/easternorthodox_1.shtml#:~:text=The%20Orthodox%20tradition%20developed%20from,sometimes%20called%20'Byzantine%20Christianity'.

- Title: Christianity and the Slavic Folk Culture: The Mechanisms of Their Interaction

Date Accessed: 12/8/2022

Link: https://www.mdpi.com/2077-1444/12/7/459/htm

- Title: Who Were the Mongols?

Date Accessed: 12/8/2022

Link: https://www.nationalgeographic.com/culture/article/mongols

- Title: The Mongol Threat

Date Accessed: 12/8/2022

Link: https://courses.lumenlearning.com/atd-herkimer-westerncivilization/chapter/the-mongol-threat/

- Title: Golden Horde

Date Accessed: 12/8/2022

Link: https://www.worldhistory.org/Golden_Horde/

- Title: Ivan I and the Rise of Moscow

Date Accessed: 12/8/2022

Link: https://courses.lumenlearning.com/atd-herkimer-westerncivilization/chapter/ivan-i-and-the-rise-of-moscow/

- Title: Alexander Nevsky

Date Accessed: 12/8/2022

Link: https://www.thoughtco.com/alexander-nevsky-profile-p2-1788255

- Title: Grand Duchy of Moscow

Date Accessed: 22/8/2022

Link: https://courses.lumenlearning.com/suny-fmcc-boundless-worldhistory/chapter/the-grand-duchy-of-moscow/

- Title: Ivan III of Russia

Date Accessed: 22/8/2022

Link: https://www.newworldencyclopedia.org/entry/Ivan_III_of_Russia

- Title: Why Was Ivan So Terrible?

Date Accessed: 22/8/2022

Link: https://www.history.co.uk/articles/why-was-ivan-so-terrible

- Title: Three Terrible Things Ivan the Terrible Did

- Title: Rurikid Dynasty

Date Accessed: 22/8/2022

Link: https://www.encyclopedia.com/history/encyclopedias-almanacs-transcripts-and-maps/rurikid-dynasty

- Title: Michael Romanov (Russia) (1596-1645; ruled 1613-1645)

Date Accessed: 22/8/2022

Link: https://www.encyclopedia.com/history/encyclopedias-almanacs-transcripts-and-maps/michael-romanov-russia-1596-1645-ruled-1613-1645

- Title: The Romanov

Date Accessed: 22/8/2022

Link: https://courses.lumenlearning.com/suny-hccc-worldcivilization/chapter/the-romanovs/

- Title: Peter the Great

Date Accessed: 22/8/2022

Link: https://www.rmg.co.uk/stories/topics/peter-great

- Title: Russo-Persian Wars

Date Accessed: 22/8/2022

Link: https://www.encyclopedia.com/history/encyclopedias-almanacs-transcripts-and-maps/russo-persian-wars

- Title: Peter the Great and his Legacy (1682-1762)

Date Accessed: 22/8/2022

Link: http://web-static.nypl.org/exhibitions/russia/level3.html

- Title: Peter the Great

Date Accessed: 22/8/2022

Link: https://www.biography.com/political-figure/peter-the-great

- Title: Russo-Persian War

Date Accessed: 22/8/2022

Link: https://artsandculture.google.com/entity/russo-persian-war/m0bv7gt?hl=en

- Title: Peter the Great Dies

Date Accessed: 24/8/2022

Link: https://www.history.com/this-day-in-history/peter-the-great-dies

- Title: The Brief Reign of Peter III

Date Accessed: 24/8/2022

Link: https://courses.lumenlearning.com/suny-hccc-worldhistory2/chapter/the-brief-reign-of-peter-iii/

- Title: Catherine the Great (1729-1796)

Date Accessed: 24/8/2022

Link: https://www.bbc.co.uk/history/historic_figures/catherine_the_great.shtml

- Title: How Did Catherine the Great's Reign Shape Imperial Russian History

Date Accessed: 24/8/2022

Link: https://www.thebritishacademy.ac.uk/blog/how-did-catherine-the-great-reign-shape-imperial-russian-history/

- Title: 10 Facts About the Russian Enlightenment

Date Accessed: 24/8/2022

Link: https://www.historyhit.com/facts-about-the-russian-enlightenment/

- Title: Pugachev's Rebellion: 5 Questions about the biggest uprising in Russia's history

Date Accessed: 24/8/2022

Link: https://www.rbth.com/history/326277-5-questions-about-pugachevs-rebellion

- Title: The Imperial Russian Army 1725-1796

Date Accessed: 24/8/2022

Link: https://link.springer.com/chapter/10.1007/978-0-230-10822-6_4

- Title: Orthodox Russia

Date Accessed: 24/8/2022

Link: https://www.psupress.org/books/titles/0-271-02349-X.html

- Title: Russian Northern Expeditions (18th-19th Centuries)

Date Accessed: 24/8/2022

Link: https://www.whoi.edu/beaufortgyre/history/history_russian1819.html

- Title: What Really Happened After Peter the Great Died?

Date Accessed: 24/8/2022

Link: https://www.grunge.com/716399/what-really-happened-after-peter-the-great-died/

- Title: Peter II

Date Accessed: 24/8/2022

Link: http://www.saint-petersburg.com/royal-family/peter-ii/

- Title: Why Peter the Great Tortured and Killed His Own Son

Date Accessed: 24/8/2022

Link: https://www.history.com/news/peter-the-great-tortured-killed-own-son#:~:text=But%20even%20those%20royals%20might,for%20allegedly%20conspiring%20against%20him.

- Title: The Seven Years War 1756-1763
Date Accessed: 24/8/2022
Link: https://www.thoughtco.com/the-seven-years-war-1756-1763-1222020
- Title: Jun 24, 1812 CE: Napoleon Invades Russia
Date Accessed: 25/8/2022
Link: https://education.nationalgeographic.org/resource/napoleon-invades-russia
- Title: Why Napoleon's Invasion of Russia Was the Beginning of the End
Date Accessed: 25/8/2022
Link: https://www.history.com/news/napoleons-disastrous-invasion-of-russia
- Title: Napoleon Defeated at Waterloo
Date Accessed: 25/8/2022
Link: https://www.history.com/this-day-in-history/napoleon-defeated-at-waterloo
- Title: Nicholas I of Russia
Date Accessed: 25/8/2022
Link: https://www.newworldencyclopedia.org/entry/Nicholas_I_of_Russia
- Title: The Decembrist Revolt
Date Accessed: 25/8/2022
Link: https://courses.lumenlearning.com/suny-hccc-worldhistory2/chapter/the-decembrist-revolt/
- Title: The Russo-Turkish War, 1828-1829
Date Accessed: 25/8/2022
Link: https://academic.oup.com/british-academy-scholarship-online/book/35530/chapter-abstract/305708973?redirectedFrom=fulltext#no-access-message

- Title: Poland's 'largest uprising' EVER took place 153 years ago today

Date Accessed: 25/8/2022

Link: https://www.thefirstnews.com/article/polands-largest-uprising-ever-took-place-153-years-ago-today-4354

- Title: Russo-Persian Wars

Date Accessed: 25/8/2022

Link: https://www.encyclopedia.com/history/encyclopedias-almanacs-transcripts-and-maps/russo-persian-wars

- Title: The Westerners and the Slavophiles

Date Accessed: 25/8/2022

Link: https://courses.lumenlearning.com/suny-hccc-worldhistory2/chapter/the-westerners-and-the-slavophiles/

- Title: Crimean War

Date Accessed: 25/8/2022

Link: https://www.history.com/topics/british-history/crimean-war

- Title: The Outcome of the Crimean War

Date Accessed: 25/8/2022

Link: https://www.historic-uk.com/HistoryUK/HistoryofBritain/Outcome-Crimean-War/#:~:text=On%2030th%20March%201856%2C%20the,the%20Ottoman%20Empire%20and%20Sardinia.

- Title: Alexander II of Russia

Date Accessed: 25/8/2022

Link: https://www.newworldencyclopedia.org/entry/Alexander_II_of_Russia

- Title: The Emancipation of the Russian Serfs, 1861

Date Accessed: 25/8/2022

Link: https://www.historytoday.com/archive/emancipation-russian-serfs-1861

- Title: Russo-Turkish War

Date Accessed: 25/8/2022

Link: https://www.encyclopedia.com/history/encyclopedias-almanacs-transcripts-and-maps/russo-turkish-war

- Title: U.S takes possession of Alaska

Date Accessed: 25/8/2022

Link: https://www.history.com/this-day-in-history/u-s-takes-possession-of-alaska

- Title: Czar Alexander II assassinated in St. Petersburg

Date Accessed: 25/8/2022

Link: https://www.history.com/this-day-in-history/czar-alexander-ii-assassinated

- Title: Alexander III of Russia

Date Accessed: 25/8/2022

Link: https://www.newworldencyclopedia.org/entry/Alexander_III_of_Russia

- Title: May Laws

Date Accessed: 25/8/2022

Link: https://www.encyclopedia.com/religion/encyclopedias-almanacs-transcripts-and-maps/may-laws

- Title: Review: The Franco-Russian Alliance

Date Accessed: 25/8/2022

Link: https://www.jstor.org/stable/45336751

- Title: Trans-Siberian Railroad

Date Accessed: 25/8/2022

Link: https://www.britannica.com/topic/Trans-Siberian-Railroad

- Title: Nicholas II (1868-1918)

Date Accessed: 27/08/2022

Link: https://www.bbc.co.uk/history/historic_figures/nicholas_ii.shtml

- Title: 1905 Russian Revolution

Date Accessed: 27/08/2022

Link: https://www.newworldencyclopedia.org/entry/1905_Russian_Revolution

- Title: Bloody Sunday Massacre in Russia

Date Accessed: 27/08/2022

Link: https://www.history.com/this-day-in-history/bloody-sunday-massacre-in-russia

- Title: The Duma in Russian History

Date Accessed: 27/08/2022

Link: https://www.thoughtco.com/duma-in-russian-history-1221805

- Title: Russo-Japanese War

Date Accessed: 27/08/2022

Link: https://www.history.com/topics/japan/russo-japanese-war

- Title: How World War I Fueled the Russian Revolution

Date Accessed: 27/08/2022

Link: https://www.history.com/news/world-war-i-russian-revolution

- Title: Grigori Rasputin

Date Accessed: 27/08/2022

Link: https://www.newworldencyclopedia.org/entry/Grigori_Rasputin

- Title: Russian Revolution

Date Accessed: 27/08/2022

Link: https://www.history.com/topics/russia/russian-revolution

- Title: Why Czar Nicholas II and the Romanovs Were Murdered

Date Accessed: 27/08/2022

Link: https://www.history.com/news/romanov-family-murder-execution-reasons

- Title: Vladimir Lenin

Date Accessed: 30/08/2022

Link: https://www.history.com/topics/russia/vladimir-lenin

- Title: Leon Trotsky

Date Accessed: 30/08/2022

Link: https://www.biography.com/scholar/leon-trotsky

- Title: Russian Revolution

Date Accessed: 30/08/2022

Link: https://www.history.com/topics/russia/russian-revolution

- Title: Nov 7, 1917, CE: October Revolution

Date Accessed: 30/08/2022

Link: https://education.nationalgeographic.org/resource/october-revolution

- Title: Bolsheviks Revolt in Russia

Date Accessed: 30/08/2022

Link: https://www.history.com/this-day-in-history/bolsheviks-revolt-in-russia

- Title: An Anti-Bolshevik Alternative

Date Accessed: 30/08/2022

Link: https://uwpress.wisc.edu/books/5573.htm

- Title: The Russian Civil War

Date Accessed: 30/08/2022

Link: https://courses.lumenlearning.com/suny-hccc-worldhistory2/chapter/the-russian-civil-war/

- Title: Karl Marx

Date Accessed: 30/08/2022

Link: https://www.history.com/topics/germany/karl-marx

- Title: Joseph Stalin

Date Accessed: 30/08/2022

Link: https://www.history.com/topics/russia/joseph-stalin

- Title: Formation of the Soviet Union

Date Accessed: 30/08/2022

Link: https://courses.lumenlearning.com/suny-hccc-worldhistory2/chapter/formation-of-the-soviet-union/

- Title: The New Economic Policy

Date Accessed: 30/08/2022

Link: https://alphahistory.com/russianrevolution/new-economic-policy-nep/#:~:text=The%20NEP%20replaced%20war%20communism,the%20sale%20of%20surplus%20goods.

- Title: Soviet Union

Date Accessed: 30/08/2022

Link: https://www.history.com/topics/russia/history-of-the-soviet-union

- Title: Soviet Policy on Nationalities, 1920's-1930s

Date Accessed: 30/08/2022

Link: https://www.lib.uchicago.edu/collex/exhibits/soviet-imaginary/socialism-nations/soviet-policy-nationalities-1920s-1930s/

- Title: Joseph Stalin's Show Trials: A Short Summary

Date Accessed: 30/08/2022

Link: https://www.historyonthenet.com/stalin-show-trials-summary

- Title: Great Purge

Date Accessed: 30/08/2022

Link: https://www.history.com/topics/russia/great-purge

- Title: Kronstadt Rebellion

Date Accessed: 31/08/2022

Link: https://alphahistory.com/russianrevolution/kronstadt-rebellion/

- Title: What Were Stalin's Five-Year Plans?

Date Accessed: 31/08/2022

Link: https://www.historyhit.com/first-five-year-plan-begins/

- Title: The Invasion of the Soviet Union

Date Accessed: 31/08/2022

Link: https://www.facinghistory.org/holocaust-and-human-behavior/chapter-8/invasion-soviet-union

- Title: Operation Barbarossa

Date Accessed: 31/08/2022

Link: https://www.history.com/topics/world-war-ii/operation-barbarossa

- Title: Auschwitz is Liberated

Date Accessed: 31/08/2022

Link: https://www.history.com/this-day-in-history/soviets-liberate-auschwitz

- Title: Soviets Declare War on Japan, Invade Manchuria

Date Accessed: 31/08/2022

Link: https://www.history.com/this-day-in-history/soviets-declare-war-on-japan-invade-manchuria

- Title: What Will Russia Do After the War?

  Date Accessed: 31/08/2022

  Link: https://www.nationalww2museum.org/war/articles/what-will-russia-do-after-war

- Title: Cold War History

  Date Accessed: 31/08/2022

  Link: https://www.history.com/topics/cold-war/cold-war-history

- Title: Berlin Blockade

  Date Accessed: 31/08/2022

  Link: https://www.history.com/topics/cold-war/berlin-blockade

- Title: The Warsaw Pact is Formed

  Date Accessed: 31/08/2022

  Link: https://www.history.com/this-day-in-history/the-warsaw-pact-is-formed

- Title: Cuban Missile Crisis

  Date Accessed: 31/08/2022

  Link: https://www.history.com/topics/cold-war/cuban-missile-crisis#:~:text=During%20the%20Cuban%20Missile%20Crisis,90%20miles%20from%20U.S.%20shores.

- Title: Arms Race, Space Race

  Date Accessed: 31/08/2022

  Link: https://www.khanacademy.org/humanities/whp-origins/era-7-the-great-convergence-and-divergence-1880-ce-to-the-future/x23c41635548726c4:other-materials-origins-era-7/a/arms-race-space-race

- Title: SALT Treaties

  Date Accessed: 31/08/2022

  Link: https://www.encyclopedia.com/history/encyclopedias-almanacs-transcripts-and-maps/salt-treaties

- Title: The Space Race

  Date Accessed: 31/08/2022

  Link: https://www.history.com/topics/cold-war/space-race

- Title: The Anti-Ballistic Missile (ABM) Treaty at a Glance

  Date Accessed: 31/08/2022

  Link: https://www.armscontrol.org/factsheets/abmtreaty

- Title: Nikita Khrushchev

Date Accessed: 5/09/2022

Link: https://www.history.com/topics/cold-war/nikita-sergeyevich-khrushchev

- Title: De-Stalinization

Date Accessed: 5/09/2022

Link: https://www.encyclopedia.com/history/encyclopedias-almanacs-transcripts-and-maps/de-stalinization

- Title: Stagnation in the Soviet Union

Date Accessed: 5/09/2022

Link: https://alphahistory.com/coldwar/stagnation-soviet-union/

- Title: From Sputnik to Spacewalking: 7 Soviet Firsts

Date Accessed: 5/09/2022

Link: https://www.history.com/news/from-sputnik-to-spacewalking-7-soviet-space-firsts

- Title: Mikhail Gorbachev

Date Accessed: 5/09/2022

Link: https://www.nobelprize.org/prizes/peace/1990/gorbachev/biographical/

- Title: Perestroika

Date Accessed: 5/09/2022

Link: https://www.history.com/topics/cold-war/perestroika-and-glasnost

- Title: The Chernobyl disaster: What happened, and the long-term impacts

Date Accessed: 5/09/2022

Link: https://www.nationalgeographic.com/culture/article/chernobyl-disaster

- Title: Boris Yeltsin

Date Accessed: 5/09/2022

Link: https://www.history.com/topics/russia/boris-yeltsin

- Title: Vladimir Putin

Date Accessed: 5/09/2022

Link: https://www.forbes.com/profile/vladimir-putin/?sh=5870d016fc58

- Title: Chronicles of the First and Second Chechen Wars

Date Accessed: 5/09/2022

Link: https://www.academicapress.com/node/415

- Title: Vladimir Putin

Date Accessed: 5/09/2022

Link: https://www.britannica.com/biography/Vladimir-Putin

- Title: Collapse of the Soviet Union

Date Accessed: 06/09/2022

Link: https://www.history.com/topics/cold-war/fall-of-soviet-union

- Title: Berlin Wall

Date Accessed: 06/09/2022

Link: https://www.history.com/topics/cold-war/berlin-wall#:~:text=at%20high%20speeds.-,The%20Berlin%20Wall%3A%20The%20Fall%20of%20the%20Wall,to%20cross%20the%20country's%20borders.

- Title: Pyotr Ilyich Tchaikovsky

Date Accessed: 06/09/2022

Link: https://www.britannica.com/biography/Pyotr-Ilyich-Tchaikovsky

- Title: Sergey Rachmaninoff

Date Accessed: 06/09/2022

Link: https://www.britannica.com/biography/Sergey-Rachmaninoff

- Title: Nikolai Rimsky-Korsakov

Date Accessed: 06/09/2022

Link: https://www.abt.org/people/nikolai-rimsky-korsakov/

- Title: Dmitri Shostakovich: A Life

Date Accessed: 06/09/2022

Link: https://www.classicfm.com/composers/shostakovich/guides/dmitri-shostakovich-life/

- Title: Igor Stravinsky

Date Accessed: 06/09/2022

Link: https://www.newworldencyclopedia.org/entry/Igor_Stravinsky

- Title: Leo Tolstoy

Date Accessed: 06/09/2022

Link: https://www.biography.com/scholar/leo-tolstoy

- Title: Alexander Pushkin

Date Accessed: 06/09/2022

Link: https://www.poetryfoundation.org/poets/alexander-pushkin

- Title: Fyodor Dostoevsky

Date Accessed: 06/09/2022

Link: https://www.newworldencyclopedia.org/entry/Fyodor_Dostoevsky

- Title: Maxim Gorky

Date Accessed: 06/09/2022

Link: https://www.britannica.com/biography/Maxim-Gorky

- Title: Nikolai Gogol

Date Accessed: 06/09/2022

Link: https://www.newworldencyclopedia.org/entry/Nikolai_Gogol

- Title: Anton Chekhov

Date Accessed: 06/09/2022

Link: https://www.britannica.com/biography/Anton-Chekhov

- Title: Alexander Solzhenitsyn

Date Accessed: 06/09/2022

Link: https://www.nobelprize.org/prizes/literature/1970/solzhenitsyn/biographical/

- Title: Dmitri Mendeleev

Date Accessed: 06/09/2022

Link: https://www.khanacademy.org/humanities/big-history-project/stars-and-elements/knowing-stars-elements/a/dmitri-mendeleev

- Title: Ivan Pavlov

Date Accessed: 06/09/2022

Link: https://www.thoughtco.com/ivan-pavlov-biography-4171875

- Title: Mikhail Lomonosov

Date Accessed: 06/09/2022

Link:
https://www.newworldencyclopedia.org/entry/Mikhail_Lomonosov

Printed in Poland
by Amazon Fulfillment
Poland Sp. z o.o., Wrocław
16 December 2022

171fc331-825b-4c43-80f5-2ebdc965cb2cR01